Stamping Effects
in Polymer Clay
with Sandra McCall

NORTH LIGHT BOOKS
CINCINNATI, OHIO
www.artistsnetwork.com

about the author

Sandra McCall is an artist, author and teacher who enjoys finding new ways to marry basic art supplies to rubber stamp-related products. She teaches paper arts classes in stores and at conventions across the United States and in Australia. To create her signature projects, she rubber stamps on everything from fabric and paper to polymer clay and metal, often combining several surfaces to create multimedia pieces. Her articles and artwork have appeared in all the major rubber stamping magazines, including *Belle Armoire, Expression, Somerset Studio, The Rubber Stamper* (her art made the cover of the premiere issue), *RubberStampMadness, National Stampagraphic* and *Vamp Stamp News*.

Sandy is the author of three popular rubber stamping books, *Making Gifts with Rubber Stamps*, the *30-Minute Rubber Stamp Workshop* and *Sandra McCall's Rubber Stamped Jewelry*, all published by North Light Books. In addition, she has a DVD called *Fabricadabra: Material Magic with Sandra McCall*, published by PageSage.

JudiKins and Stamp Oasis both sell stamps made from Sandy's original drawings. Check out their online catalogs to see more of Sandy's artwork.

Stamping Effects in Polymer Clay with Sandra McCall. Copyright © 2006 by Sandra McCall. Manufactured in China. All rights reserved. The patterns and drawings in the book are for personal use of reader. By permission of the author and publisher, they may be either hand-traced or photocopied to make single copies, but under no circumstances may they be resold or republished. It is permissible for the purchaser to make the projects contained herein and sell them at fairs, bazaars and craft shows. No other part of this book may be reproduced in any form or by any electronic or mechanical means including information storage and retrieval systems without permission in writing from the publisher, except by a reviewer, who may quote a brief passage in review. Published by North Light Books, an imprint of F+W Publications, Inc., 4700 East Galbraith Road, Cincinnati, Ohio 45236. (800) 289-0963. First edition.

10 09 08 07 06   5 4 3 2 1

Library of Congress Cataloging-in-Publication Data

McCall, Sandra
  Stamping effects in polymer clay with Sandra McCall.-- 1st ed.
    p. cm.
  Includes index.
  ISBN-13: 978-1-58180-763-9
  ISBN-10: 1-58180-763-5
  1. Polymer clay craft. 2. Handicraft. I. Title.
TT297.M375 2006
745.57'2--dc22
                                2005029038

Distributed in Canada by Fraser Direct
100 Armstrong Avenue
Georgetown, ON, Canada L7G 5S4
Tel: (905) 877-4411

Distributed in the U.K. and Europe by David & Charles
Brunel House, Newton Abbot, Devon, TQ12 4PU, England
Tel: (+44) 1626 323200, Fax: (+44) 1626 323319
Email: mail@davidandcharles.co.uk

Distributed in Australia by Capricorn Link
P.O. Box 704, S. Windsor, NSW 2756 Australia
Tel: (02) 4577-3555

Editor: Jessica Gordon
Designers: Stephanie Goodrich and Brian Roeth
Layout Artist: Kathy Gardner
Production Coordinator: Greg Nock
Photographers: Christine Polomsky, Tim Grondin
Stylist: Nora Martini

F+W PUBLICATIONS, INC.

metric conversion chart

TO CONVERT	TO	MULTIPLY BY
Inches	Centimeters	2.54
Centimeters	Inches	0.4
Feet	Centimeters	30.5
Centimeters	Feet	0.03
Yards	Meters	0.9
Meters	Yards	1.1
Sq. Inches	Sq. Centimeters	6.45
Sq. Centimeters	Sq. Inches	0.16
Sq. Feet	Sq. Meters	0.09
Sq. Meters	Sq. Feet	10.8
Sq. Yards	Sq. Meters	0.8
Sq. Meters	Sq. Yards	1.2
Pounds	Kilograms	0.45
Kilograms	Pounds	2.2
Ounces	Grams	28.3
Grams	Ounces	0.035

Dedication

There are so many people who have influenced me in the polymer clay field. From the miniature artists who inspired me to make a ton of tiny baubles for my dollhouse all the way through to the artists who showed me that clay is not just for kids, I have been inspired, amazed and awed.

In alphabetical order: Judy Belcher, Mike Buesseler, Kathleen Dustin, Steven Ford and David Forlano, Gwen Gibson, Lindly Haunani, Tory Hughes, Donna Kato, Karen Lewis (Klew), Barbara McGuire, Peggy-Jo Palmer, Lisa Pavelka, Nan Roche, Judith Skinner, Pier Voulkos, Lisa Ward—it is with appreciation and humility that I dedicate this book to you.

Acknowledgments "No man is an island." Who first said that? Ummm… "I have not been raised in a cave." OH! I know who said that one! It was Karen Thomas! Both quotes are so true and so appropriate of creativity! I think that very few of us artists have been raised in a cave. We get inspiration, knowledge and empowerment from each other almost daily. I want to thank every creatively positive person who has crossed my path because I know you are the reason that I continue trying to live the creative life.

Thanks also go to my family members, all of whom are wonderfully creative people.

As always, I thank and appreciate the people who take my classes as well as the store owners and the event promoters who allow me to teach at their venues.

Thanks to my editor, Jessica Gordon. Not only are you incredibly organized and thoughtful, but what fun you are!

Thanks to my photographer, Christine Polomsky, who is a doll and a delight in addition to being a photo-pro!

Thanks to the team at North Light. I pass the word on to everyone who wonders about which publisher to work with. You guys are the BEST!

Finally, thanks to my product suppliers: Clearsnap, Inc., Dharma Trading Co., Hero Arts, Jacquard Products, JudiKins, Polyform Products, Plaid Enterprises, Post Modern Design, Stampotique, Van Aken (Kato Polyclay). I sincerely could not afford to do very much in the way of book writing if it were not for your continued generosity.

inside

Jewelry
22

Personal Accessories
56

Home Accessories
80

Introduction

Polymer clay is enjoying another bout of popularity, due in part to several new advances in the industry. Polymer clay artists and manufacturers are coming up with some great new products that make polymer clay even easier and more fun to work with than ever before. For instance, there's a fairly new clay called Kato Polyclay that, once baked, is more flexible and stronger than clays previously on the market, making it perfect for buttons, handles and other clay pieces with stress joints. Polymer clay artist Lisa Pavelka has also come out with Poly Bonder, a new super glue that can be baked in the oven to create a strong bond even between baked and unbaked polymer clay. Another great new product is Liquid Polyclay, developed by Van Aken International, that is thinner and therefore clearer than previous liquid clays. Van Aken also has a product called Repel Gel that keeps uncured clay from sticking to itself during the baking process.

The advent of these products caused me to look at polymer clay with fresh eyes and new excitement. I discovered that when you blast polymer clay with a heat gun after it has been cooked, you can create great shine without sanding and buffing! Yeah! That quick little trick alone made me love polymer clay all over again. (Can you tell I did not like the sanding and buffing process?)

I have been inspired by the advances in the polymer clay world to develop some new techniques with rubber stamped polymer clay that I think you'll enjoy exploring. For a helpful guide to these 16 special effects, refer to the Sampler Sneak Peek (page 18). I've also included an extensive resource listing to help you find everything you need. There are helpful tips spread throughout the pages and lots of extra information on the mediums used in each project. Finally—and perhaps most importantly—in the pages that follow, you'll find 25 original projects and variations for making great jewelry, personal accessories and items for your home.

Whether you're a beginner or an advanced polymer clay artist, I hope you'll find something cool, useful or inspiring in this book. Now let's go play clay!

Polymer Clay [Basics]

Working with polymer clay really does invite play and exploration. Don't stress about whether you're doing things "right" or not. Just learn as you go. On these pages you'll find some information that's useful to have as you begin—maybe you can avoid some of the mistakes I made when I was just starting out.

working with clay

Always work on a clean, non-porous surface, like a flexible piece of vinyl paper, ceramic tile or glass. I like vinyl paper because I can simply bend it to remove the clay. I also sometimes use cardstock if I am moving the clay directly into the oven on the cardstock.

While it's hard for me to take my own advice to keep my work surface clean, I do try—it really shows in the final product. Use a wet wipe to periodically clean your work area, clay rollers and tools. Clean the pasta machine's rollers by rolling a wet wipe through the machine.

conditioning clay

All polymer clay must be conditioned before it's used. Old, unworked clay starts to separate into its chemical components. Once baked, it is brittle and breaks easily, if not conditioned properly.

You can condition clay with a pasta machine or with your hands. In either case, start by slicing ⅛" (3mm) pieces off the block, or slices a little wider than the thickest setting on the pasta machine.

Before rolling old clay through the machine, you must soften it. Do *not* force too thick, too large or too hard a slab of clay through the machine. The gears are made of a kind of plastic, and it is

If, as you condition the clay, you get air bubbles, slice the bubbles with a tissue blade and then smooth the flap down with your fingers.

very easy to strip them if the clay is too thick or too hard. Soften the clay with the heat from your hands by holding it between your palms for a minute or two. You can also soften clay with a heat gun. Give it just a tiny bit of heat—too much and the clay will start to cure. If the clay is still too hard, smooth a small coating of Liquid Polyclay onto the raw clay, wrap it in plastic wrap and let it sit for half an hour. Then, continue to work the clay, blending the liquid clay with the solid.

When using a pasta machine, roll the clay through at least 20 times. Clay is fully conditioned when the edges of the slab are smooth (not broken up like they are in the first couple of passes).

If you condition clay with your hands, roll the clay, fold it over, twist and roll it again between your palms. Repeat until the clay is soft and workable. To determine if the clay is well conditioned, form a clay ball and flatten it. If the edges are broken and jagged, keep conditioning the clay until it is smooth and pliable.

storing clay

The first thing I learned, way back when, was that polymer clay bonds with some kinds of plastic. I found out this little gem the hard way when I stuck an open package of clay into a little plastic drawer. When I went back for the clay, it had become one with the drawer. Avoid this scenario by storing clay in plastic baggies or by wrapping it in plastic wrap. The same goes for scrap clay. I throw mine into a big baggie. If you must store your clay in a hard plastic container, check it by placing a little raw clay on the plastic. If the clay sticks after an hour, don't use it for storage.

Also steer clear of storing clay in or on paper or wax paper, as the clay's plasticizers leech into the paper, making clay brittle and hard to condition.

baking clay

Bake in a well-ventilated area! Polymer clay fumes are non-toxic when clay is baked per package directions, but the fumes can be irritating.

Baking temperatures and times may vary from oven to oven. Heating elements are usually on the bottom of the oven, so place the tray on the highest rack, farthest away from the heating element. Since my oven (and most toaster ovens) comes up to a certain degree, shuts off and then kicks in again as the oven cools, there are heat spikes during baking. Preheat the oven until the elements are not red hot—watch while cooking and turn the knob down just a hair to stop the elements from getting red hot again. Bake test pieces according to package instructions, and adjust temperature and baking times accordingly. I like to bake my clay at 250°F (121°C) for 15 minutes per ¼" (.6cm) of clay. If you overcook clay, it will bubble, turn blackish-brown and get very brittle. Burning releases toxic fumes, so take the piece outside to cool and then toss it.

Polymer clay mimics the surface sheen of the material on which it is baked. For instance, cardstock gives baked clay a dull, matte finish, while glass or sleek metal creates a very shiny, glassy finish.

When making a flat clay piece—like a polymer painting (see page 85) or a brooch—flatten it as it cools by placing it on a piece of cardstock, covering it with another sheet of cardstock and weighting it with a stack of magazines or some other weight.

This "Bakelite" pin was first blasted with a heat gun to achieve a shine and then I rebaked it, face down on cardstock. You can see that the surface now has a dull coat while the impressions of the stamp remain glossy. Pretty cool, huh?

mixing clay colors

I mix clay colors with one part intuition and one part color mixing knowledge. I've been mixing paint for practically my whole life, so it's quite easy for me to color match by eye. However, I know many of my students are not as comfortable. If you fall into this category, take heart. Van Aken's polymer clay (Kato Polyclay) and Polyform Products (Sculpey III, Premo!) are very close to true artist's colors, so you'll achieve consistent results. You'll also be able to mix according to the color wheel (red plus yellow equals orange, yellow plus blue equals green, and so on) and get the expected results. If color is not artist quality, then red and yellow may equal a kind of putty-colored orange instead of the clear, beautiful orange you expect.

When making the first batch of a mixed color, write down how much of one block you use of one color and how much of another, and you'll be able to duplicate the color easily. I know, it's a pain in the neck to keep a record, but if you fall into the "unsure-how-to-mix-color" category, then you should consider this little step.

using a heat gun with polymer clay

Use a heat gun to cure small pieces of clay quickly or to bring up the shine on pieces coated with liquid polymer clay without rebaking. You may also set ink with a heat gun, but only when you are satisfied with the shape of the piece.

Make sure you do not get so close to the clay with a heat gun that it bubbles and burns. Keep the heat gun moving over the clay as you bake it.

cleaning up

Use alcohol to clean your work surface of clay and dye. Alcohol also cleans liquid polymer clay off of baked clay, and cleans unbaked clay off of baked clay. It's great for removing dried acrylic paint from baked clay and from your tools.

For your hands, use a pumice cleanser or a hand cleaner for removing dyes. My favorite hand cleaner is ReDuRan—it contains both light pumice and dye remover.

What [You'll Need]

You really don't need mountains of stuff to create the beautiful polymer clay projects in this book. Gather the basic supplies listed on these pages—some clay, a few cutters and clay blades, some ink and paint—and you'll be ready to go.

polymer clay

Polymer clay comes in lots of different colors and in different forms, including liquid form. Different brands of clay have different properties and may lend themselves to particular types of projects.

SOLID CLAY

The two clays that I use almost exclusively are **Kato Polyclay** and **Premo!** At least one of these is almost always available in any craft store today. Of the two clays, Kato clay is more flexible once baked and is easier to cut with scissors. However, you may soften any baked clay with a heat gun to make it easy to cut. If you have a project where you need to flex the clay to glue it onto a shape such as a slightly rounded hairclip, then Kato clay is your best bet. Baked Premo! clay also shapes well when reheated.

LIQUID CLAY

Liquid Polyclay and **Liquid Sculpey** are brand names for liquid polymer clay. Polymer clay in liquid form can be used to glue unbaked pieces of polymer clay together. The clay does not set until after it's baked. Liquid clay may also be used as a smoother (put a little on your finger to smooth away seams and fingerprints). When wet, liquid polymer clay looks milky white, but after baking it is clear and shiny. Mix it with re-inkers to make a clay "paint." Mix it with mica powder and oil paint to make the raised texture in "lampwork" beads. Liquid clay can be used to soften clay during conditioning and as a finishing coat.

tools for cutting and making impressions in clay

To give clay shape and texture, you'll need a selection of rubber stamps, clay blades, brayers and clay cutters. There is a huge selection of both rubber stamps and clay cutters. Start with a few of each, and build your collection as you go.

Clockwise from left to right: Marxit clay ruler, acrylic roller, circle clay cutter, clay blades, clay punches, polymer clay, rubber stamps

)) **Rubber stamps** come in all shapes and sizes and in a wealth of images and patterns. Generally, the deeper the etching on a rubber stamp, the more expensive it is. Deeply etched stamps create better impressions in clay.

)) An **acrylic roller** or **brayer** is a solid plastic cylinder that works like a rolling pin. Use it to flatten clay.

)) **Clay blades** are straight-edge blades used to cut clay. I use several different types of blades, including the tissue blade, the flex blade and the straight blade. The tissue blade is sharper than the other blades and is good for precision cutting. The flex blade is for cutting rounded shapes and the more rigid straight blade is for cutting cane slices or for cutting into a block of clay.

)) **Clay cutters** are small metal shapes used to cut clay shapes. These range from cutters made especially for clay to cookie cutters.

)) A **Marxit** is a six-sided clay ruler with incremental markings along each side invented by polymer clay pioneer Donna Kato. Use it to cut clay into pieces of consistent thickness. See the photo on page 15 for how to use this tool.

supplies for making clay stick and shine

When finishing up clay pieces, you'll often need to adhere components together and also apply a coat of varnish. Below I've listed my favorites.

POLYMER ADHESIVES

Zap-A-Gap is my favorite cyanoacrylate glue (super glue) for attaching baked pieces of clay together. You must not bake any piece with super glue on it as there is some concern with toxicity. You can use Liquid Polyclay or Liquid Sculpey as a glue if the piece is to be baked.

There is also a new super glue created by Lisa Pavelka that can be baked. You can order the glue from Lisa's website, which is listed in the resource guide (page 124).

gadgets for conditioning and curing clay

You'll need just a few larger-ticket items for working with clay (although you can get by without them, if necessary). A heat gun, a toaster oven and a pasta machine will prove invaluable if you've been bitten by the clay bug.

» A **heat gun** is a small, powerful electric heat source used to dry paint and ink, to set embossing powders, to cure clay, to soften clay, and to blast baked clay for a high shine.

» A **toaster oven** is a small oven useful for baking clay. Dedicate the oven to clay and crafts once you have baked polymer clay in it.

» A **pasta machine** is invaluable for rolling very flat sheets of clay. It makes conditioning and blending clay a lot faster, too. I found that, even if you buy the more expensive machines, they still have the same old plastic gears inside and will go bad just as fast as the less expensive machines if you mishandle them.

FINISHING COATS FOR CLAY

Apply a **gloss coat** to clay to protect the surface of the clay and to add shine. Plaid's Treasure Crystal Cote is the thickest, shiniest coating that I know of without the mess of a two-part epoxy. Acrylic varnishes, Krylon Low Odor Clear spray in matte or gloss coat, Flecto Varathane varnish, Diamond Glaze and embossing powder will all work well for coating clay. Do NOT use lacquer! That means no nail polish for polymer clay. It will just stay tacky to the touch forever.

Clockwise from left to right: re-inkers, embossing powder, inkpads, Krylon clear gloss spray, colored pencils, permanent marker, Galaxy marker, Zap-A-Gap, Treasure Crystal Cote, paints

paints, powders and inks for coloring clay

Clay is remarkably receptive to color from different mediums, including paints, embossing powders, inks and some kinds of markers. Start your collection with a few of your favorite colors, and expand on it as necessary.

» **Acrylic paint** adheres well to polymer clay and comes in a wide variety of colors. I use Plaid's Metallic paint as well as the Folk Art colors.

» **Embossing powders** add luster and dimension to clay. Sprinkle them onto clay and then bake or melt the powder with a heat gun to set it.

» **Ink** is great for stamping, blending into translucent clay and mixing with liquid polymer clay. Ink comes in a variety of colors, including metallics. For the projects in this book, I use inkpads, re-inkers and alcohol inks.

» **Markers** are a simple way to add color to clay. I use gel pens, metallic pens, Krylon pens, permanent markers, permanent ink pens, and Galaxy Markers.

Polymer Clay [Techniques]

You don't need to know everything about polymer clay to get started. If you master just a few simple techniques, you'll be able to build from there—before you know it, you'll be a polymer clay maestro!

Conditioning Clay with a Pasta Machine

Conditioning clay with a pasta machine is much easier than conditioning by hand, especially if you have a machine with a motor. If there is no motor (I don't have one yet), it is still faster than conditioning by hand. Remember that once you have used polymer clay on a pasta machine, it must be dedicated exclusively to crafts from then on. Do not use a pasta machine for food if it has touched polymer clay.

step2

RUN CLAY SLICES THROUGH PASTA MACHINE

After you've sliced several pieces of clay, layer them next to each other so they overlap slightly and press the slices together. Run the staggered clay vertically through the pasta machine on the thickest setting.

step1

CUT CLAY INTO SLICES

Use a straight clay blade to cut a block of clay into ⅛" (3mm) thick slices, or just a little thicker than the thickest setting on the pasta machine.

step3

CONTINUE TO ROLL CLAY THROUGH PASTA MACHINE

After running the staggered clay pieces together through the pasta machine a few times, fold the sheet in half to make it shorter and run it through the pasta machine fold side first. Make sure to fold the clay in half carefully so that the sides match up as evenly as possible.

DON'T
Don't feed the clay with the slices placed horizontally. This will trap air and cause tiny bubbles to form all throughout the clay.

DON'T
Don't run the clay through the pasta machine with the folded edge at the top. Again, the clay will develop huge air bubbles.

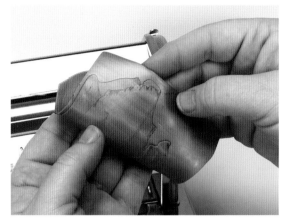

step4

MAKE SURE THERE ARE NO RIDGES

When you pass a folded piece of clay through the pasta machine, one side will show the fold and the other side will be smoother and will have fewer ridges. Fold the smoother sides together for the next pass through the pasta machine. Even rolling the ridged sides together can cause tiny air bubbles to form.

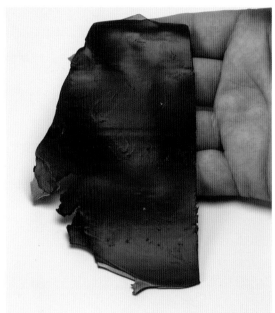

helpful **tip** The image at right shows what can happen as a result of mixing unconditioned clay with conditioned clay. One was much softer than the other, so after folding and rolling several times, you can see a ton of tiny air bubbles. This will show up in the baking process and make your piece look unattractive.

Conditioning Clay by Hand

Although a pasta machine does make conditioning clay faster and easier, conditioning clay by hand is very simple too. You definitely do not have to own a pasta machine to play with clay.

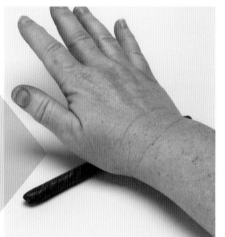

step1

ROLL CLAY INTO SNAKE

To condition clay without a pasta machine, roll it into a snake between your hands. Continue rolling the clay on your work surface.

step2

TWIST CLAY

After rolling the clay into a snake, fold and twist it. Repeat the rolling, folding and twisting process. Your goal is to blend the clay ingredients as well as to make the clay warmer and more malleable for your modeling.

Making a Bead from Scrap Clay

You can make beautiful marbled beads from scrap clay. Simply grab a ball of any color scrap clay or pinch together a few hand-selected colors. Either way, each bead will be different and just as cool as the one before.

step1

TWIST SCRAP CLAY

Take a lump of scrap clay and form it into a thick log shape. Twist the log of clay multiple times.

step2

SMOOTH OUT SNAKE, FOLD AND TWIST AGAIN

Smooth out the twisted surface so it is a longer snake. Fold the smooth snake in half and twist it again.

step3

ROLL CLAY INTO BALL

Roll the clay into a ball about 1" (3cm) in diameter. (The size of the ball will depend on how much clay you started with.)

step4

CUT BALL INTO THIN SLICES

Use a tissue blade to cut the clay ball into about three or four slices, again depending on the size of the clay ball.

step5

THIN OUT SLICES

Run one slice at a time through the pasta machine, beginning at the thickest setting and stepping it down to a medium-thick setting.

step6

COVER SCRAP CLAY BALL

Use more of the scrap clay ball to form another ball. Cover the scrap clay ball with two of the prettiest slices that were run through the pasta machine.

step7

SMOOTH EDGES

Roll the covered ball around in your hands to smooth out the edges.

helpful tip Sometimes you will want to make beads that are consistent in size, regardless of whether you are working with scrap clay or not. Roll a snake of clay to the thickness that you like. Use a Marxit clay ruler to make measured impressions in the clay. Simply slice the clay at each of the impressions made by the tool and then roll the beads into the desired shape.

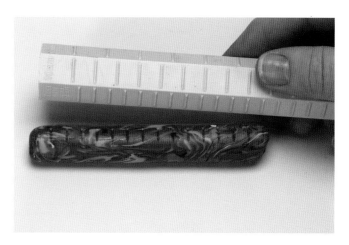

Cutting Canes

When cutting canes or when cutting a round slice of clay off a snake, it's important not to distort the circular shape. To cut a smooth slice that allows the colors and patterns in the cane to keep their integrity, simply maintain a slight rotating motion as you cut through the cane.

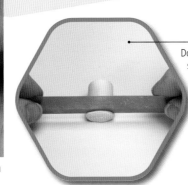

DON'T

Don't push the clay blade straight down through the cane. Slicing a cane straight down from top to bottom compresses the design of the cane and distorts it.

As you slice a cane, use the clay blade to roll the cane gently on your work surface so the blade cuts through the clay from side to side, rather than straight through from top to bottom.

Baking on Clay Piers

You will, on occasion, want to keep a clay piece, such as a bead or other round object, off the baking surface as it is cured in the oven. A simple way to make sure that rounded pieces keep their rounded shape is to make little scrap clay piers. After your piece is baked, so are your piers—and you can then use them over and over.

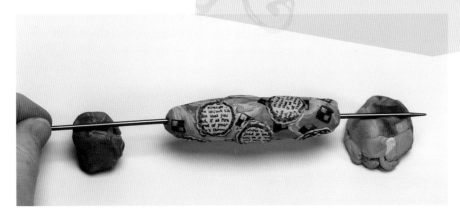

To construct scrap clay piers, simply form two hunks of scrap clay into flat-bottomed mounds. Stick a skewer through the center of your bead and impress both ends of the skewer into the tops of the scrap clay mounds to make slight indentions.

Odds (and Ends)

As you complete your polymer clay projects, you'll probably start asking yourself a couple of questions: What do I do with all of this leftover clay? Is this thing really finished—maybe I should make it shiny? This information will help you answer these burning questions...

scrap clay

The pieces of clay that you cut away from your working project are scrap clay. Keep all of your scrap clay—it always comes in handy. For example, use scrap clay to make little piers for baking beads and things, as a core to cover with fresh clay, and to make pretty marbled beads. You can also grab a hunk to use as a third hand when you need to keep something steady. You'll find all kinds of uses for scrap clay, so don't throw it away!

Keep all of your scrap clay together in a big pile. (I keep mine in a large plastic baggie.) Each time you cut a piece of clay from a project, stick it on top of the stack. Just dip into your stash whenever you need a bit of extra color.

to gloss or not to gloss

That is the question that will come to you now and then. I add a gloss coat to my piece if the work calls for it in my eyes. There is no right or wrong—just do whatever appeals to you.

UNGLOSSED CLAY
An unglossed clay surface can be effective, especially if you are working on a piece that should look primitive, earthy or just matte in finish.

GLOSSED CLAY
This bowl has been glossed with Plaid's Treasure Crystal Cote. Glossing can give a more finished look to some projects.

17

Sampler [Sneak Peek]

Each of the projects in this book highlights a featured technique that creates a unique texture and/or color effect. In the following pages, you'll get a sneak peek at some of my favorite techniques, along with some useful information about them, such as what they're called and a summary of how to make them. If you're especially ambitious, you might consider taking an afternoon to make sampler sheets using these techniques. Sampler sheets are great to have on hand when you're making projects. They're sort of like background papers for stamping projects. To make a sampler sheet, decorate a slab of clay with any technique you like. Roll it to the thinnest setting on the pasta machine and bake it for about seven minutes. Remove it from the oven, place it on a sheet of cardstock, place another sheet of cardstock on top of the clay piece and weight it down with a stack of magazines to flatten it as it cools.

[acryle gane one]
Stamp all over a sheet of clay with permanent ink, making a slight impression. Paint over the stamped surface with diluted acrylic paint. Let the paint dry. Run the sheet of clay through the pasta machine, bake it and let it cool.

[acryle gane two]
Make a deep impression in a sheet of clay with an uninked stamp. Rub mica powders over the stamped clay. Wash diluted acrylic paint over the clay and let it dry. Run the clay sheet through the pasta machine, bake it and let it cool.

[imitative mokume gane]
Press different colors of clay sheets together tightly until you have a stack about 2"(5cm) high. Impress objects into the clay stack. Slice thin layers off the clay stack with a clay blade, flip them over and drop them onto a clay sheet of contrasting color. Brayer over the slices of clay to adhere them to the base sheet. Run the slab through the pasta machine, bake it and let it cool.

[stained glass]
Stamp a white sheet of clay with an inked stamp and bake it. "Paint" the baked piece with a mixture of Liquid Polyclay and Clearsnap's Vivid re-inkers. Cure the clay with a heat gun. Coat the entire sheet with Plaid's Treasure Crystal Cote (or a two-part epoxy) to make the clay super-shiny and glass-like.

(**elegant elements**)

Use permanent ink to stamp an image into unbaked clay. Cut the image out with a knife or scissors. Brush it with mica powder, shape it and bake it on a bed of fiberfill.

(**colored pencil transfers**)

Stamp a thin white sheet of clay with permanent ink. Stamp a black image onto a sheet of thin, white copy paper. Color the backside of the image with colored pencils. Burnish the image, pencil-side down, onto the clay to transfer the color. Bake the clay sheet with the paper still in place. Let the clay cool, and then peel off the paper. Coat the clay sheet with Liquid Polyclay and cure it with a heat gun.

(**almost metallic leafing**)

Impress an uninked stamp into a sheet of dark clay. Paint metallic gold acrylic paint on top of the impression (don't get paint into the crevices). Let the paint dry. Flatten the piece to crack the paint. Bake the sheet and let it cool.

(**translucent stampings**)

Stamp with permanent ink all over a very thin sheet of translucent clay and let the ink dry. Wrap the clay, stamped-side down, around a core bead. Bake the covered bead and let it cool. Sand the piece with wet/dry sandpaper to smooth it. Blast it with a heat gun to bring up the shine.

(acrylic stampings)

Use a foam brush to apply acrylic paint to a rubber stamp. Stamp the image onto a sheet of clay and let the paint dry. Run the stamped clay through the pasta machine, bake it and let it cool.

(pearly whites)

Stamp a piece of pearl clay with an uninked stamp and bake it. Mix micro pearls powder with Liquid Polyclay and a drop of straw-colored ink. Paint the baked and stamped pearl clay with the mixture and let the mix settle into the crevices left from the rubber stamp. Cure the clay with a heat gun to bring up the shine.

(not canes, but canies)

With permanent ink, stamp an image onto a very thin sheet of clay. Let the ink dry and then cut out the image. Circle cutters will give a good cane imitation. Simply adhere the circles to a piece of clay, just as you would adhere actual cane slices.

(ancient images á la Gwen Gibson)

Stamp an image onto a piece of paper and make a laser photocopy of it. Turn the image right-side down on top of a sheet of clay and burnish it onto a sheet of unbaked clay. Wait 30 minutes. Rip the paper off the clay and bake the clay. Paint with acrylics and rub off the top layer of paint before it dries completely. Leave the clay unvarnished for an ancient look.

(simply impressive)

This is clay stamping at its most basic. Roll conditioned clay into a slab. Ink a stamp with any permanent ink and press it into the clay, making a slight impression. Lightly brush the top of the rubber-stamped impression with mica powder.

("painting" with clay)

Stamp with permanent ink onto different colored clay slabs. Cut out the images and apply them to a clay "canvas" until you have completed a clay "painting." Flatten the painting with an acrylic roller or by rolling it through the pasta machine, bake it and flatten it while cooling.

(collage clay under glass)

Roll a thin sheet of clay (use the thinnest setting on your pasta machine) and stamp onto it with permanent ink. Let the ink dry. Cut the images out. Turn the piece of glass so that the right side is facing your work surface. Apply the images to the glass, stamped-side down so that the images will show through the glass. Build layers as you go. Bake the piece and let it cool.

(lampwork elements)

In small squeeze bottles with fine tips, pour one part Liquid Polyclay to one part Liquid Sculpey. Mix in a pinch of mica powder and a dab of oil paint that is similar to the color of the mica powder. Heat a clay bead with your heat gun, and then draw on the surface with the colored liquid clay mixtures. Cure the clay with a heat gun.

Jewelry

I'm excited about the jewelry section of this book because I am still a miniaturist at heart. I love working on a small, intricate scale. Each wearable jewelry piece is relatively small, so every project is fast and fun to make. A huge plus is that you get to work with beads, wire and other cool stuff, in addition to working with clay. It's also easier to try a new technique on a small area rather than tackling a huge project the first time you try a particular technique.

Some of the techniques used in the jewelry projects have been passed on to me by my clay heroes. It is awesome how people can generate such original and inspiring ideas. In some cases, it is the skill of a particular artist that brings a technique to the attention of the clay community. In other cases, however, there are techniques whose originators are unknown to me, as the techniques have been passed on multiple times and have been slightly altered by each artist who uses them. Then, of course, many polymer clay artists are using the same tools and supplies and often come up with similar ideas at the same time. It is interesting to trace the origins of each technique as it comes into common use, and I will provide that information where I can. Of course, pinpointing the origin of a particular technique can be a bit like tracking folklore back to its source—it's never straightforward or simple.

Don't be afraid to put your own personal spin on any of the techniques offered here. Who knows—you might just become someone's clay hero!

brown polymer clay

ivory polymer clay

black polymer clay

previously baked ivory-colored sampler sheet (I've used the malachite sheet outlined in the Shapely Sampler project, page 30)

crinkled copper wire pieces

pin back

primitive images stamp (**STAMPOTIQUE**)

spiral stamp (**STAMP OASIS**)

text stamp

black inkpad (**STAZON**)

white acrylic paint

dark brown acrylic paint

brown permanent marker

small paintbrush

craft knife

scissors

pin vise with drill bit large enough for wires

300-grit wet/dry sandpaper

white paper

bowl of water

fiberfill

Zap-A-Gap

featured technique

ancient images á la Gwen Gibson

H i s t o r y
Lesson

Since polymer clay sticks to the toner from laser prints, you can stamp or draw an image and then make a laser photocopy of it and transfer it to the clay (inkjet prints or dye photocopies will not work). Talented polymer clay artist Peggy-Jo Palmer learned this technique from Gwen Gibson's Ancient Images video and passed it on to me in turn. One side note here: the copyrighted images of stamp companies belong to them or their artists. To protect their artwork, some stamp companies absolutely forbid photocopying of their images even if you own the stamp and have hand-stamped them. Check to be sure it is all right for you to copy your stamped images. Of course, you know not to photocopy images out of a stamp catalog, right? That is just naughty behavior.

step 1

STAMP PAPER AND MAKE COPY

Use black ink to stamp the large primitive images stamp and the spiral stamp onto white paper. Make a laser toner photocopy of the stamped images.

step 2

BURNISH IMAGES ONTO CLAY

Lay the laser printer copy of the primitive images face down onto an unbaked sheet of brown clay that has been run through the pasta machine at the thickest setting. Burnish the sheet by rubbing your finger over it until the paper is well adhered to the clay. Let the sheet sit on top of the clay for 30 minutes. Repeat this step with the spiral image onto a sheet of ivory clay.

step 3

CREATE RAGGED IMPRESSION IN CLAY

When the paper begins to look waxy, it is ready to be removed. Rip the laser copies off of both the brown and the ivory clay sheets to leave a ragged impression in the clay—the faster you rip, the better.

step 4

STAMP TEXT

Use scissors to cut a small, rectangular piece (about 1" x 2" [3cm x 5cm]) from a previously baked sampler sheet (I use an ivory malachite sampler sheet). If you can find a nice ragged edge for one side of the piece, all the better. Use black ink to stamp text onto the sampler sheet.

step5

PAINT HIGHLIGHTS ONTO STAMPED IMAGES

Cut out the spiral image with a craft knife. Bake the cut-out shell and the sheet stamped with primitive images at 250°F (121°C) for ten minutes. Flatten the pieces while cooling. To give the spiral piece an antiqued finish, squirt a puddle of brown paint directly onto the spiral and use a paintbrush to work the paint into the pattern on the clay. While the paint is still wet, rub off the excess with a paper towel, a soft cloth or your fingers so that the pattern is highlighted by the dark paint.

step6

SAND PAINT OFF OF CLAY

Use a paintbrush to cover the entire brown sheet of clay with a thin coating of white paint and let it dry. When the paint is completely dry, sand most of it off with 300-grit wet/dry sandpaper, so that the impressions left by the transfer are covered in white. Continuously dip the sandpaper and the clay piece into a bowl of water as you sand.

step7

ATTACH BAKED PIECES TO CLAY BACKING

Cut the sanded piece of brown clay to a piece about 1" x 2" (3cm x 5cm) to create the backing for the pin. Color the edges of the clay pieces with a brown marker. Use Zap-A-Gap to attach all of the pieces to the backing, layered as shown.

step8

THREAD COPPER WIRE THROUGH HOLES

Drill a few small holes into the clay piece with a pin vise. Thread copper wire pieces through the holes to make it appear that the layers in the pin are held together only by the primitive wire.

step9

COVER WIRES WITH CLAY SHEET

To cover the exposed wires on the backside of the pin, cut a piece of clay off a thin sheet of previously baked black clay to just a bit smaller than the pin. Cut two slits in the black clay, thread a pin back into it and glue it to the backside of the brooch.

To finish the pin, apply a fresh sheet of black clay as a pin backing and stamp impressions in it to alleviate that oh-so-lumpy look. Then you can rebake the piece, face down, on a bed of fiberfill at 250°F (121°C) for 15 minutes.

- white polymer clay
- pearl polymer clay
- Liquid Polyclay
- fine silver chain necklace
- 2" (5cm) of fine silver chain
- two crystal beads
- one seed bead
- one pearly bead
- 3" (8cm) 22-gauge silver craft wire
- three silver jump rings
- sun mask rubber stamp (JUDIKINS)
- straw-colored Vivid re-inker (CLEARSNAP)
- paintbrush
- round-nose pliers
- needle-nose pliers
- wire cutters
- heat gun
- pin vise with small drill bit

featured technique

pearly whites

Pearly Whites
Necklace

This fine-lined sun mask image is perfect for a small delicate necklace like this. I wanted to make the polymer clay look like "pearls" so I played around with the mica powders and the Diamond Glaze and re-inkers. It didn't come out looking exactly like a pearl, but I like the effect.

step 1

STAMP SUN MASK ONTO MIXED WHITE AND PEARL CLAY

Stamp the uninked sun mask stamp onto a sheet of mixed white and pearl clay that has been rolled through the thickest setting on the pasta machine. Bake at 250°F (121°C) for ten minutes and let it cool.

step 2

INK STAMPED IMPRESSION

Cut out the sun face with a clay blade. Mix a few drops of re-inker with Liquid Polyclay and brush it onto the stamped image of the face. Let the ink settle into the stamped impression.

 helpful **tip** Heat guns make quick work of curing clay and setting ink, but you do have to take some care when using one. Be sure to keep the heat gun moving to avoid bubbles in the clay, and don't get too close or you'll burn the clay. Practice curing clay on a scrap sheet to avoid any mishaps before you actually move on to one of your good projects.

step 3

CURE LIQUID POLYCLAY WITH HEAT GUN

Use a heat gun to cure the Liquid Polyclay and to make it shiny. Let it cool completely. Add a second coat of Liquid Polyclay and cure it with the heat gun again. Let the piece cool completely before handling.

step4

DRILL HOLES IN PENDANT

Drill two small holes at the base of the pendant and one hole at the top.

step5

CRIMP ONE END OF SILVER WIRE

Cut a 3" (8cm) length of silver wire and make a tiny crimp at one end by using round-nose pliers, gripping the very tip of the wire with the very tip of the pliers and twisting up.

step6

ATTACH BEADS

Thread a seed bead, a crystal bead, a pearl bead and another crystal bead onto the wire with the crimp at the end. Attach the beaded dangle to the middle of the small chain. Use jump rings to attach the chain to the two holes at the bottom of the sun face.

step7

ATTACH JUMP RING

Attach a jump ring at the top of the pendant and thread the necklace through it.

white polymer clay

cream polymer clay

black polymer clay

translucent polymer clay

Liquid Polyclay

previously baked sampler sheet

pin back

text stamp (STAMP OASIS)

black inkpad (STAZON)

template

paintbrush

craft knife

clay blade

heat gun

straight edge

credit card or piece of chip board

Zap-A-Gap

featured technique

stamped malachite

Shapely
Sampler

Donna Kato made a pin using this construction technique at one of her demos several years ago. It was the first time I had ever seen her up close and in "real life." I'm such a huge fan of hers that I was totally starstruck. All I could sputter out was, "I love your work." And then I ran.

At least I wasn't too shy to admire her work! Donna uses cut pieces of her decorated clay pressed onto a thin clay sheet and then surrounds the pieces with a clay border for a sophisticated mosaic look. I loved her technique and thought I could put my own spin on the process by using my sampler sheets and cutting the pin into a really cool, freeform shape.

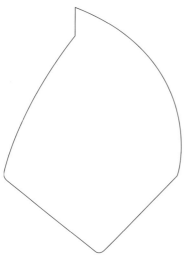

PATTERN SHOWN AT FULL SIZE.

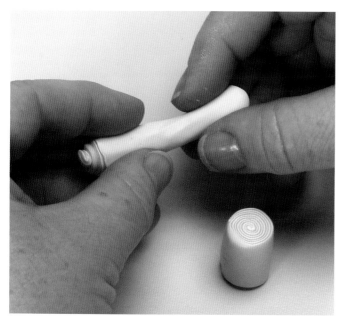

step1

ROLL UP STACKED AND THINNED CLAY

Roll a small amount of white polymer clay through the pasta machine at a medium-thick setting. Repeat with the cream and translucent clay. Stack all three sheets and run them together through the pasta machine at the thickest setting. Cut the sheet in half and stack the two halves. Roll them through the pasta machine at the thickest setting. Repeat cutting and stacking once more, so that the sheet has 12 total layers. Roll up the stacked sheets of clay from one end to the other into a bull's eye cane.

step2

CUT AND REDUCE CANE

Use the clay blade to cut the cane in half. Reduce one half of the cane by pinching and pulling it, beginning in the middle and working out toward the ends.

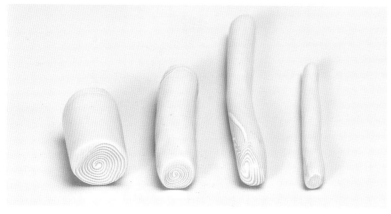

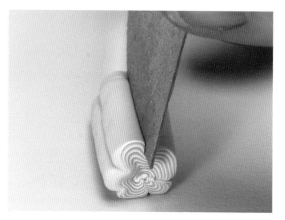

step3

REDUCE CANE FURTHER

Cut the cane in half again and reduce one half of it. You will have four different-sized canes.

step4

MAKE INDENTATIONS IN CANE

Use a credit card or a piece of chip board to make indentations into the sides of the three larger canes. Make about six indentations all the way around each cane.

step5

ADHERE CANES TOGETHER

Squish all of the canes together to form an irregular malachite-like formation.

step6

CREATE CLAY SHEET FROM CANE SLICES

Slice ⅛" (3mm) pieces from the cane. Lay all of the pieces next to each other on your work surface, pinching them together as you work. Once completed, run the sheet through the pasta machine on a medium-thin setting.

step7

STAMP MALACHITE SHEET

Stamp the malachite sheet with the text stamp using a black permanent inkpad. Bake the stamped sheet at 250°F (121°C) for seven minutes and weight it to flatten it as it cools.

step8

CREATE DECORATIVE ELEMENTS

Choose a coordinating pre-baked sampler sheet. Use a shapelet to trace and cut out one element from the sampler sheet and one element from the malachite sheet. Cut the elements in half using a straight edge and a craft knife.

step 9

CREATE SHAPE AND BORDER

Roll a small piece of black clay through the pasta machine at a medium-thin setting for the base of the pin. Place one half of one element on the black clay sheet and place one half of the other element next to it, lining up the straight edges. Cut two ½" to 1" (1cm to 3cm) strips from a medium-thin sheet of black clay to create the border. Wrap one strip around one half of the shape. Use your clay blade to make a straight vertical cut through the clay strip starting at the point of the shape. Repeat with the other strip for the second side. Smooth the seam together with your fingers.

step 10

TRIM BORDER

Use a clay blade to cut around the border to form the pin shape. You may cut the shape freehand or follow the template on page 31. Smooth the fingerprints from the black clay and bake it at 250°F (121°C) for 15 minutes.

step 11

FINISH PIN

Coat the piece with Liquid Polyclay and blast it with the heat gun to cure it. Add a pin back with Zap-A-Gap.

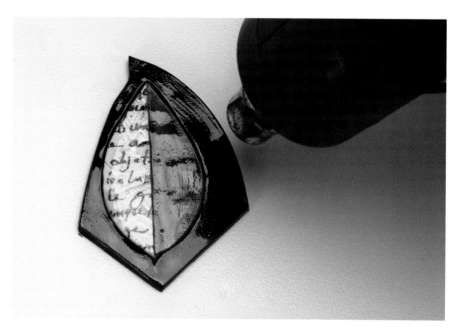

charcoal grey polymer clay

previously baked beige sampler sheet and additional sampler sheets

short piece of black leather cord

text rubber stamps (STAMPER'S ANONYMOUS)

texture rubber stamp (STAMPOTIQUE)

rubber stamps on sampler sheet (JUDIKINS)

black inkpad (STAZON)

gold mica powder

red mica powder

dark blue acrylic paint

low-gloss acrylic medium

small paintbrush

craft knife

tissue blade

Zap-A-Gap

pin back

featured technique

acrylic stampings

Memories

Isn't the phrase on this text stamp so pretty? It says it all. You can let the words take center stage, or add to their beauty with further embellishments, if you like. For the cord inlay, you could just as well use a black polymer clay snake, or think about using fiber, beads, sequins or whatever else strikes your fancy. Look through your "stuff" bins—I'll bet you have a ton of really cool stuff you can use to dress this pin up even more if you want.

step 1

STAMP TEXT ONTO CLAY AND CUT BASE SHAPE

Roll a sheet of charcoal grey clay through the pasta machine at the thickest setting. Cut a small rectangular piece of cured, beige sampler sheet and stamp text onto it. Place it and a coordinating piece of previously baked sampler sheet onto the grey clay. Use a tissue blade to cut the grey clay into the desired base shape for your pin.

step 2

CUT CLAY

Use a craft knife to cut around the small sampler sheet pieces. Carefully lift out the sampler sheet pieces and peel the uncooked clay from their backs.

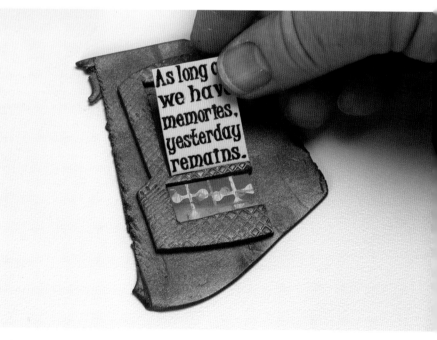

step 3

STAMP IMPRESSIONS INTO CLAY

With an uninked stamp, make impressions on the front of the cut piece of grey clay.

step 4

PLACE BAKED CLAY PIECES

Roll another small piece of grey clay through the pasta roller at the thinnest setting. Lay the cut piece of grey clay on top of the thin sheet of grey clay and insert the baked pieces into the open slots.

step 5

ADD COLOR TO PIN

Trim the bottom piece of grey clay to the same size as the top piece. Use a small paintbrush to brush on gold and red mica powders. Dilute dark blue acrylic paint with water and apply a wash of color over the pin. Let the paint dry completely. Bake at 250°F (121°C) for 15–20 minutes.

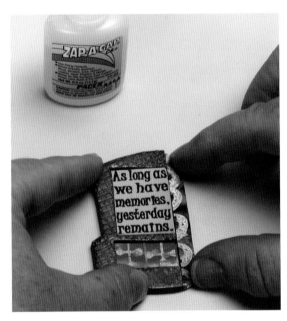

step 6

ADD SAMPLER SHEET TO BROOCH

Glue a slice of previously baked sampler sheet into place onto the side edge of the brooch with Zap-A-Gap.

step 7

ADHERE LEATHER CORD

Use Zap-A-Gap to adhere a piece of thin black leather cord onto the seam between the grey clay and the side sampler sheet.

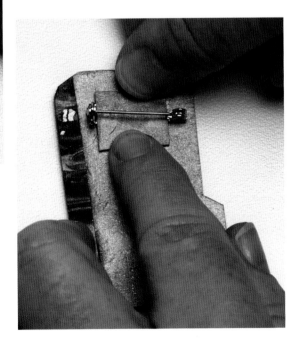

step 8

FINISH PIN

Use Zap-A-Gap and a small piece of previously baked sampler sheet to attach the pin back. Coat the pin with low gloss acrylic medium if you wish.

materials

black polymer clay

green polymer clay

gold metallic clay

Liquid Polyclay

previously baked mokume gane
sampler sheet and/or various
other sampler sheets

two small gold beads

two pre-made pearly clay beads

2" (5cm) piece of brass-colored
craft wire

pin back

leaf rubber stamp (**JUDIKINS**)

dot stamp (**HERO ARTS**)

black inkpad (**STAZON**)

gold mica powder

paintbrush

craft knife

tissue blade

brayer

thin knitting needle

round-nose pliers

wire cutters

fiberfill

Zap-A-Gap

featured technique

imitative mokume gane

Leafy
Leanings

Here's an easy way to create mokume gane while making use of what polymer clay artists call the mica shift properties of metallic polymer clay. It was on a DVD of Mike Buesseler's beautiful work that I was first introduced to "mica shift" in polymer clay. When I tried to find the originator of this concept, I was told that it was most likely Pier Voulkos. But if you ask Pier, she says that many artists happened upon this idea at the same time. All this is to say that I did not think up the mica shift concept, but I am glad that someone did!

Don't worry, mica shift properties are not technical or confusing. It's just a term for how mica flecks in polymer clay are going in all different directions. If you roll clay and flatten it through the pasta machine, then you are lining up the mica in one direction. When you make an imprint or cut the clay and lay a sheet on top of another sheet in a different direction, then you will see a lighter or darker color—kind of like the pile on velvet or carpet.

step1

STACK CLAY AND MAKE IMPRESSIONS

Roll a large sheet of gold metallic clay through the pasta machine at the thickest setting. Cut the clay sheet into four equal pieces and stack them. Press a small dot stamp all over the stacked clay. Also poke a small knitting needle through the stacked clay repeatedly.

step2

LAYER GOLD PIECES ONTO BLACK CLAY

Roll a small sheet of black clay through the pasta machine at the thickest setting until you have a piece that is about 2"x 3" (5cm x 8cm). Cut very thin slices from the gold stack of clay and flip them over so that the "top" side is face down as you layer them on top of the black square of clay.

step3

ADHERE GOLD SLICES TO BLACK CLAY

Brayer over the clay sheet lightly using an acrylic roller to make sure the gold pieces are adhered. Roll the sheet of clay through the pasta machine at the thickest setting, and continue to step down two levels on the pasta machine until you reach the thinnest setting.

step4

CREATE BLACK BORDER FOR GOLD PIECE

Cut the mokume gane sheet into the shape you desire, using the tissue blade to create a curved edge at the top. Roll a small sheet of black clay through the pasta machine at a medium thickness. Place the mokume gane sheet on top of the black sheet of clay. Cut two thin strips of black clay to create borders, and place them along the top and bottom edges of the gold piece.

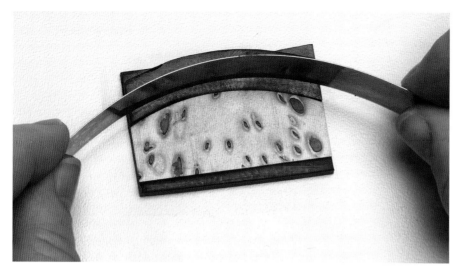

step 5

TRIM EDGES AND SMOOTH

Trim the black clay and the border strips to the desired size. Smooth the edges if necessary and smooth away any fingerprints. Bake the piece at 250°F (121°C) for 15–20 minutes.

step 6

CREATE LEAF

Run a small sheet of green clay through the pasta machine at a medium-thin setting. Stamp a leaf image onto the clay sheet and cut it out with a craft knife. Brush the leaf with gold mica powder and shape it so that it has movement. Bake it on a bed of fiberfill and let it cool.

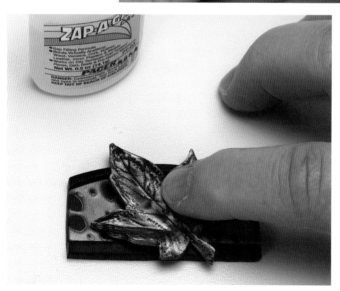

step 7

ADHERE LEAF TO BROOCH

Adhere the leaf to the brooch with Zap-A-Gap.

step 8

FINISH PIN

Crimp one end of a small piece of brass-colored craft wire and thread on one small gold bead, two pearly beads and another small gold bead. Clip the wire and crimp the end closed. Attach the wire assemblage to the front of the leaf with Zap-A-Gap. To finish, secure the pin back to the piece with a small sampler piece of clay and Zap-A-Gap.

materials

dark brown clay

previously baked sampler sheet

variety of beads and sparkling fibers

crimped copper wires

pin back

primitive figure stamp (**IMPRESS ME**)

textured abstract square stamp (**JUDIKINS**)

bronze embossing powder

copper, green, red and gold metallic acrylic paints

paintbrush

craft knife

small circle clay cutter

tissue blade

heat gun

hot glue gun

Zap-A-Gap

featured technique

imitative raku

Rakuvian
Brooch

If you like the look of fired Raku ceramics, then I think you'll have fun experimenting with this technique. The imitative secret is embossing powders and dry-brushed metallic acrylic paints. This little figure looks both ancient and futuristic—a fitting contradiction for a Raku piece.

40

step1

CUT SHAPES FROM CLAY

Roll a piece of brown clay through the pasta machine at the thickest setting. Stamp the primitive figure image and the square image onto the clay sheet and cut around them. Cut out two circles about ½" (1cm) in diameter from the brown clay and cut out a hole in the center of each one with a clay cutter, roughly in the center. Bake all of the pieces at 250°F (121°C) for ten minutes.

step2

DRYBRUSH CLAY CUT-OUTS

Drybrush the metallic acrylic paints over each piece. To drybrush, dip a small paintbrush into the paint color without wetting the brush, and wipe off any excess paint on a paper towel or a scrap piece of paper. Run the brush over the pieces to leave light streaks of color. Repeat with all of the colors for each piece.

step3

CURE EMBOSSING POWDER WITH HEAT GUN

Sprinkle bronze embossing powder over the paint and cure it with the heat gun to make it look like a fired Raku glaze. There is no need to wait for the paint to dry before moving on to this step.

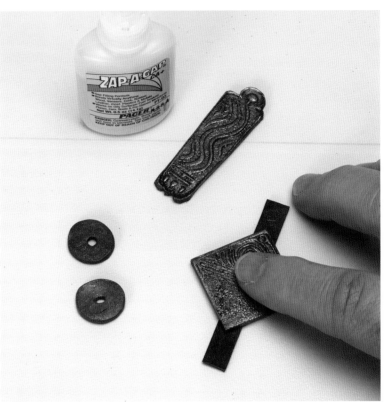

step4

CHECK CLAY BACKING FOR LENGTH

Determine the length of your pin by laying out the primitive figure shape with a circle directly above and below it. Cut a small strip of the baked clay sampler sheet that will be long enough to accommodate the three pieces without covering up the holes in the circles (you will be tying fibers through the holes in a later step).

step5

ADHERE SQUARE

Adhere the square diagonally to the backing strip with Zap-A-Gap. Turn the backing strip over and adhere another square of the same size diagonally to the backside of the strip, overlapping the square on the front so that just a little of the back square shows on the front (see step 6).

step6

TIE ON SPARKLING FIBERS

Tie the sparkling fibers onto the circles with a slip knot and trim the ends to about ¼" (6mm). Glue the circles onto the strip of backing above and below the square.

step 7

GLUE ON WIRES

Cut five pieces of crimped copper wire. Lay them on the front of the base pin piece. Put hot glue on the backside of the primitive figure. Press the figure onto the pin piece, trapping the wires between the layers.

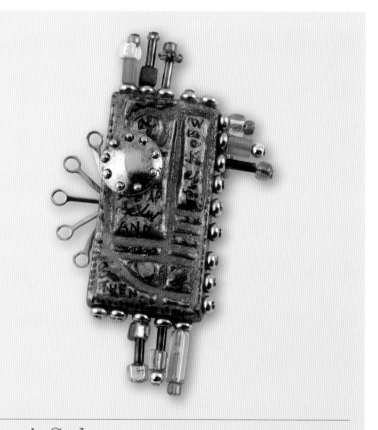

step 8

FINISH PIN

Bead and curl the wires in a funky, haphazard manner, making sure to crimp the ends to secure the beads. Glue a pin back onto the back of the piece with a small square of sampler sheet and Zap-A-Gap.

Circuit Style The stamp used on this pin looks kind of like a circuit board when dressed with all the brass beads and other odds and ends from my "stuff" bins. Throw all your old or broken jewelry into your "stuff" bin. Then you can rummage through it to add to your clay pieces as needed. The side spokes on this piece are craft wire and beads and were added after baking. Drill small holes, put a drop of glue into the hole and then insert the beaded wire with Zap-A-Gap.

materials

- white polymer clay
- silver polymer clay
- Liquid Polyclay
- previously baked sampler sheet
- small square silver-colored beads
- silver spacers to fit the square beads
- 18–20 gauge silver craft wire
- pin back
- sunshine rubber stamp (STAMPERS ANONYMOUS)
- dots stamp (HERO ARTS)
- black inkpad (STAZON)
- blue, yellow and lime green dye re-inkers (CLEARSNAP VIVID)
- silver embossing powder
- permanent marker
- medium gloss acrylic varnish (TREASURE CRYSTAL COTE)
- paintbrush
- craft knife
- tissue blade
- wire cutters
- heat gun
- hot plate or hot pot for melting embossing powder
- pin vise with small drill bit
- small aluminum pan
- Zap-A-Gap

featured technique

stained glass

Sunny Stained
Glass Brooch

Full of colors bursting forth like a day at the sea, this sunny brooch is as easy to make as it is to wear. The Treasure Crystal Cote is a thick, glossy top coat. If you let the first coat dry completely and then add a second, you will get a very good glass-like appearance. If you have a Suze Weinberg hot pot to melt your silver powder, lucky you! Use it for this project instead of an aluminum pan.

step1

STAMP IMAGE AND CUT OUT

Roll a sheet of white clay through the pasta machine at the thickest setting. Stamp the sun image onto the clay sheet with black ink. Cut out the stamped image and separate part of the image with a tissue blade as shown. (To make one brooch, you'll need just one half of the stamped image.)

ING

at a

sheet with an

the back of

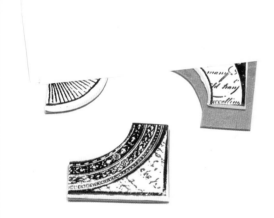

step3

CUT AROUND WHITE CLAY CUT-OUTS

Flip the silver sheet of clay over and place the stamped sun pieces on top of it. Trim the silver clay along the edges of the white clay pieces. Bake the stacked pieces at 250°F (121°C) for 15 minutes.

step4

APPLY COLOR TO WHITE CUT-OUTS

Mix one drop blue re-inker with about ¼ teaspoon of Liquid Polyclay. Repeat with yellow and lime green re-inkers. Paint the stamped and cut-out images with the colored mixture. Let the color flow so that you will have a smooth, glass-like look. Bake the painted pieces at 250°F (121°C) for ten minutes. Let cool.

step5

EMBOSS EDGES OF COLORED CLAY PIECES

Use a small aluminum pan over a hot plate to melt a pile of silver embossing powder. You may heat the powder on the stove over very low heat or use a low airflow heat gun. Dip the edges of each piece of the pin into the melted powder and let cool. Repeat this step until every edge of every piece has been embossed with the silver powder.

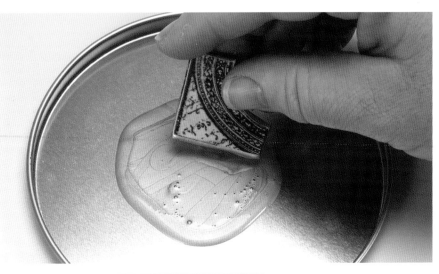

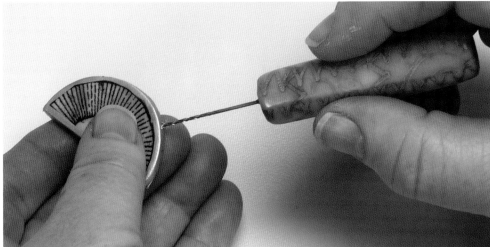

step6

DRILL HOLES IN EDGE OF SUN CUT-OUT

Drill tiny holes along the rounded edge of the sun cut-out with a pin vise. The holes should be spaced about ¼" (6mm) apart to create six holes, leaving about 1½" to 2" (4cm to 5cm) in the center with no holes.

step7

ATTACH WIRE SPOKES TO SUN

Cut six 1" (3cm) pieces of silver craft wire. Put a dab of Zap-A-Gap in one of the drilled holes. Feed a wire spoke into one hole. Repeat until all six wire spokes are in place.

step8

BEAD WIRE SPOKES

Dab a little glue onto a spoke, then thread on a spacer, a bead and another spacer. Repeat for the remaining spokes. Let the glue dry. Lay the side pieces of the pin next to the beaded piece and mark the spots where the wire touches them with a permanent marker.

step9

ATTACH CLAY PIECES TO WIRE SPOKES

Drill holes at the spots you marked. Dab glue in these holes to securely to attach the center piece of the brooch.

step10

APPLY VARNISH

Brush a thick coat of clear varnish (Treasure Crystal Cote) onto the face of the "stained glass." Let it dry completely.

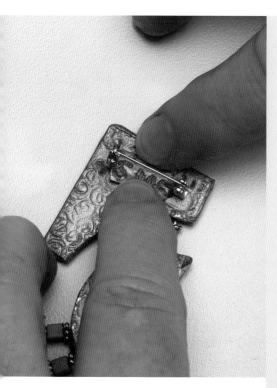

step11

FINISH PIN

Attach the pin back with Zap-A-Gap. Then cut a small piece of previously baked sampler sheet and glue it to the pin support with Zap-A-Gap.

Rooster-Eyes Stained Glass Pin Isn't this the coolest rooster stamp ever? This rooster's know-it-all attitude makes me laugh. This pin is made with the same process as the Sunny Stained Glass Brooch, but the separately embossed pieces are then glued to a previously baked clay sheet used as a backing to hold them all together. Find this stamp from Picture Show.

materials

- pale beige polymer clay
- scrap polymer clay
- Liquid Polyclay
- assorted small beads in black, gold, copper and ivory
- flat disk beads
- seed beads
- 20" (51cm) and 24" (61cm) of gold linen beading cord
- 24" (61cm) of thin black cord
- small square checkerboard rubber stamp (**HERO ARTS**)
- circle text stamp (**STAMP OASIS**)
- black inkpad (**STAZON**)
- gold metallic acrylic paint
- paintbrush
- craft knife
- needle tool
- skewer
- scissors
- 1" (3cm) circle cutter
- heat gun
- pin vise with small drill bit
- paper towel or soft cloth
- Zap-A-Gap

featured technique

not canes, but canies

Writing in
Circles

For this primitive and personality-packed accessory, you will want to plow through your scrap clay and pick a bead-sized pinch in a color range that you like. Mine is in the beige tones, but just about any color of scrap clay will work for this design. Once you've picked out your clay, you get to rummage through your beads. This is a great project for using up leftover beads from other projects.

step1

STAMP SCRAP CLAY BEAD

Make a large tubular bead with beige scrap clay (see Polymer Clay Techniques, page 14). Slide a skewer longways through the bead and hold onto one end. Stamp all over the bead with the small checkerboard stamp.

step2

STAMP AND CUT OUT WORDY CIRCLES

Roll a small piece of pale beige clay through the pasta machine until you reach the thinnest setting. Stamp the clay sheet with wordy circles using black ink. Cut around each circle using a circle clay cutter, scissors or a craft knife.

step4

BUILD CLAY PIERS FOR BAKING

Use two small piles of scrap clay as clay piers to rest the bead on as it bakes. Bake it at 250°F (121°C) for 15 minutes. Let the bead cool and bake it again at 250°F (121°C) for another 15 minutes to help prevent cracking due to the thickness of the bead.

step3

POKE INDENTATIONS AROUND CIRCLES

Gently press the clay circles onto the large bead. Impress tiny holes around the edges of each circle using a small skewer or any other object that's handy.

step5

PAINT BEAD GOLD

Paint the entire bead with a thick coat of gold paint. Use a paper towel or a soft cloth to wipe off the gold paint, leaving the gold color in the indentations made in step three. Allow the paint to dry. Coat the bead with Liquid Polyclay and blast it with the heat gun to cure it. Let it cool.

step6

DRILL HOLE THROUGH BEAD

Drill a hole vertically through the middle part of the bead with a pin vise.

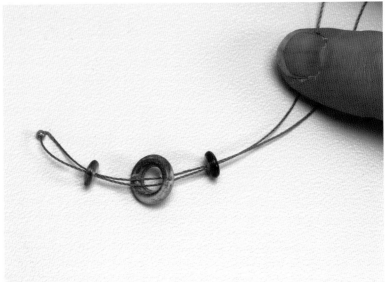

step7

CREATE BEAD CORD

Cut a 20" (51cm) length of gold beading thread and coat each end of the strand with Zap-A-Gap. Let the glue dry and then cut the ends into points to make "needles."

step8

BEGIN BEADING

Slide a seed bead onto the middle of the 20" (51cm) length of gold beading cord. After stringing on the seed bead, thread both strands through a flat disk bead, an ivory bead and another disk bead. Thread both strands through the middle hole in the big bead.

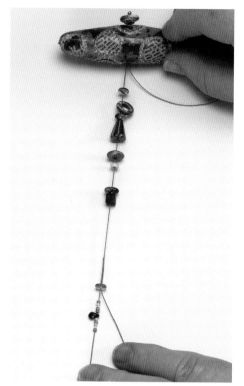

step9

MAKE DANGLES

Separate the two cords. Thread a variety of small beads onto one cord to create a 3" (8cm) dangle. Add three seed beads at the end of the dangle and then thread the cord back up through all of the beads to finish the dangle.

step10

WRAP CORD AROUND BEAD

Thread enough seed beads onto the free strand of cording to wrap around the core bead two times. (I use about 6" [15cm] of seed beads.) Wrap the beaded cord around the core bead two times, bringing the cord first to the right side of the top beads and then to the left so the cord crosses over itself.

helpful **tip**

If you'd like, you may use a beading needle instead of gluing and cutting the cord ends.

step11

SECURE WRAPPED CORD

Continue wrapping the unbeaded cord around the core bead two more times, as before, coming around once on the right side and once on the left side of the top stacked beads. Tie the two strands of cord together directly under the hole in the bead. Secure the knot with Zap-A-Gap and let it dry.

step 12

KNOT ENDS OF CORDS

On the remaining lengths of cord, string the beads as shown, beginning with seed beads and ending with several larger beads. Knot the end of each cord and secure the knots with Zap-A-Gap. Trim the excess cord.

step 13

BEAD GOLD CORD

Tie a knot about 3" (8cm) from the end of a 24" (61cm) length of gold beading cord. Slide on a grouping of beads (about 1" [3cm] of beads) and tie another knot in the beading cord to secure. Tie another overhand knot about 1" (3cm) from the first grouping of beads and string on another grouping. Continue in this manner until there is 3" (8cm) of beading cord remaining. Tie the black cord with an overhand knot to the gold beading cord in between each bead grouping. Continue to the last bead grouping.

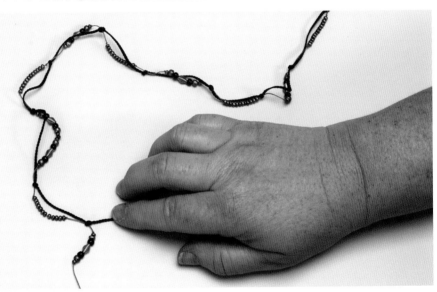

step 14

SECURE CORD INSIDE BEAD

Apply Zap-A-Gap to the ends of the gold beading cord and to the end of the black cord and press them together to make one cord. Let the glue dry. Apply glue to the hole in one side of the bead and push the end of the cords into the hole. Let dry. Repeat the process to attach the other end of the cord in the remaining hole.

black polymer clay
gold polymer clay
Liquid Polyclay
baked sampler sheet (STAMP
FROM JUDIKINS)
seed beads
four leaf beads
four small crimp beads
twisted nylon beading cord
necklace clasp (OPTIONAL)
patterned stamp
mica powder
copper metallic acrylic paint
blue metallic acrylic paint
fine-tip pen
shapelet
paintbrush
craft knife
tissue blade
thin knitting needle
scissors
crimping tool
fiberfill
Zap-A-Gap

featured
technique

**acryle gane
two**

Lazy
Lariat

The technique used on the sampler piece is so much fun. It will turn out differently every time you make it, so make a large piece in case it turns out fabulously and then you can use it for lots of projects. The crossed cord construction at the front of this necklace reminds me of a lariat. It's fast and easy enough to make for swaps if you wanted to do so.

helpful **tip**

It's economical to make several small, tubular beads at a time. Mark even increments with a Marxit if you need the beads to be all the same size. Set the excess beads aside to be used at a later date.

step1

CREATE SAMPLER SHEET

Roll a sheet of gold clay through the pasta machine at the thickest setting and stamp it with an uninked stamp. Dilute copper and blue metallic acrylic paint with water. Brush copper paint over the clay with a paintbrush, followed by a wash of blue acrylic paint. Let the paint dry completely and then run the sampler sheet through the pasta machine. Bake it at 250°F (121°C) for 7 minutes.

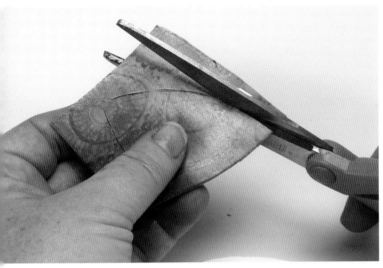

step2

CUT SHAPE FROM SAMPLER SHEET

Use a shapelet to trace a curved triangle shape onto the baked sampler sheet with a fine-tip pen. Cut the piece out with scissors.

step3

CREATE FRAME FOR CUT-OUT CLAY PIECE

Roll a sheet of black clay through the pasta machine at a medium-thin setting. Brush the back of the cut-out piece from the sampler sheet with Liquid Polyclay and center it on the piece of black clay. Cut strips of black clay and place them around the triangle shape to create a frame. Use a tissue blade to trim away the black clay, leaving a small, 1/8" (3mm) border around the triangle shape. Smooth the edges and remove fingerprints. Bake at 250°F (121°C) for 15 minutes. Flatten while cooling.

step4

WRAP CLAY AROUND KNITTING NEEDLE

Roll a black sheet of clay through the pasta machine at a medium-thin setting. Trim the clay into a narrow strip that will fit snugly around the knitting needle. Wrap the clay around the knitting needle to create a tube. Roll the covered knitting needle back and forth on your work surface with the palm of your hand to smooth out the clay.

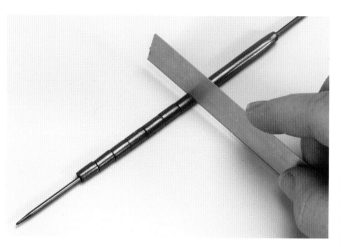

step5

CUT TUBE INTO BEADS

Brush the tube with mica powder in a color that coordinates with the sampler sheet you created. Cut the tube into several beads by rolling the clay blade and the knitting needle simultaneously to make the cuts. Bake the beads on a bed of fiberfill at 250°F (121°C) for 15 minutes. Keep the knitting needle in place while the clay is baking.

step6

ADHERE TUBE BEAD TO PENDANT

Slide the baked beads off of the knitting needle. Glue one of the tube beads onto the pendant with Zap-A-Gap. Scratch the clay with a craft knife on both the bead and the pendant before applying the glue to create a better bond.

step7

BEAD CORDS

Cut two 48" (122cm) pieces of twisted nylon cord. Put Zap-A-Gap on each end of the cords, let it dry and cut the ends into points to create "needles." String 36" (96cm) of one piece of cording in any way you like. Leave about 6" (15cm) free on either end of the cord. Pass one end of the cord through the tube bead that is glued to the front of the pendant. String on beads to form a dangle. At the end of the dangle, string on a crimp bead, three seed beads, a leaf drop and three more seed beads. Slip the end of the cord through the crimp bead to form a loop at the end of the dangle. Crimp the crimp bead tightly with a crimping tool. Slip the end of the cord up through a few more beads and secure the end with a dab of Zap-A-Gap. Clip the excess end of the cord.

step8

FINISH DANGLES

Run the other end of the cord through the tube bead and create another dangle. Repeat for the other 48" (122cm) length of nylon cord. There will be four dangles in total.

Personal Accessories

You'll find a wide and wonderful selection of accessories in this part of the book. In truth, I was dragged, kicking and screaming, from making massive amounts of jewelry into making "something other than jewelry." In spite of myself, it turned out that I had a lot of fun with these projects. You'll find a little bit of everything in this chapter—from a nature-inspired clip for your hair to a key ring with muted designs. I am especially excited about the purse project in this section. I really stumbled onto something cool when I discovered a way to make polymer clay "Bakelite" that I used for the bag's handles and buttons. Of course, now I want to do more jewelry—a whole book on Bakelite jewelry! Check out the variation Bakelite pin (see page 9) if you're thinking about making some jewelry yourself with that great imitative technique.

In the pages that follow, you'll also find lots of other great accessories, including custom tools such as drills, needle tools and awls. When you work with polymer clay, you use these tools over and over—so why not make them pretty? You'll also find tips on wire working, plus a project showing you how to make a polymer clay box. Of course, there is more, much more, so read on and have fun!

materials

- black polymer clay
- red polymer clay
- turquoise polymer clay
- blue polymer clay
- Liquid Polyclay
- thin black cording
- abstract figure stamp (**POST MODERN DESIGN**)
- sentiment stamp (**POST MODERN DESIGN**)
- black inkpad (**STAZON**)
- gold Mica Magic inkpad (**CLEARSNAP**)
- gold gel pen
- medium gloss acrylic varnish (**TREASURE CRYSTAL COTE**)
- paintbrush
- craft knife
- small circle clay cutter
- heat gun

featured
technique

**simply
impressive**

Labels of
Love

Stamped with a sentiment on each of their backsides, these tiny tags make wonderful gift tags, bookmarks or additions to your journals and cards. If you're very ambitious and if you have enough time, these would make adorable labels for your handmade gifts. Especially if you sell your work—they could be your own personal seal of excellence attached to your product. For a rubber stamp, you could carve your own design in lino blocks or have your logo made into rubber through a manufacturer. Wouldn't that be great product recognition for you?

step1

STAMP TAG BACKING

Roll out a small slab of black clay to a medium setting on the pasta machine. Stamp an uninked primitive image into the clay. Use the craft knife to cut around the stamped image, leaving a border that is slightly bigger than the image. Punch a small hole in the top of the clay with a circle clay cutter. It's easy to make several of these tags at the same time, if you like.

step2

STAMP SENTIMENT ON TAG BACK

Flip the clay over and stamp a sentiment on the back with gold Mica Magic ink.

step3

TEXTURIZE CLAY

Texturize the front of the clay piece with an uninked stamp, imprinting over the image from the first stamp. Bake the clay piece at 250°F (121°C) for 10 minutes.

step4

STAMP COLORED CLAY

Roll a thin slab of colored clay through the pasta machine at the thinnest setting and stamp the same primitive image onto it with black ink. Use the craft knife to cut around the image, staying close to the stamped line.

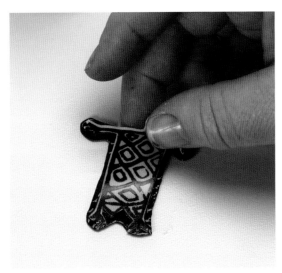

step5

ADHERE COLORED CLAY TO BLACK BACKING

Spread liquid polymer clay on the black piece of clay and adhere the smaller figure to it. Top with a sheer coat of liquid polymer clay. Slip the piece back into the oven and bake it at 250°F (121°C) for about seven minutes. Flatten while cooling.

step6

ADD GOLD DETAIL

Brush medium gloss acrylic varnish onto the back side of the tag and let it dry. Use a gold gel pen to add detail to the front of the little figure. Dry the ink with a heat gun.

helpful tip

If you're making lots of polymer clay pieces, you can shape them and then put them aside on a baking pan until you're ready to bake a lot of pieces at the same time. I usually bake my clay on a piece of cardstock or a bed of fiberfill placed on a baking sheet.

step7

THREAD FIGURE ONTO CORD

Thread the figure onto the black cording with a slip knot and tie the ends in a simple overhand knot.

materials

- ivory polymer clay
- scrap polymer clay
- Liquid Polyclay
- patterned rubber stamps (HERO ARTS)
- inkpads in garnet, green and cobalt blue (ANCIENT PAGE)
- yellow acrylic paint
- paintbrush
- tissue blade
- tapestry needle
- pliers
- heat gun
- Zap-A-Gap

featured technique

acryle gane one

Custom
Tool Set

In your craft work, and especially in clay work, you will use many tools, such as an awl, a few small drills with different-sized bits, and a variety of needle tools. So, why not make totally cool custom tools? Small handles work better for these tools because of the way you hold them against your palm and push down. When you make your handles, grab a hunk of clay and shape it to fit your hand. You can determine the size by holding the handle as if you were working with the tool. The step-outs in this project illustrate creating a needle tool.

step 1

STAMP IVORY CLAY

Run a piece of ivory clay through the pasta machine at a medium setting. Stamp it with various overlapping stamps in different colors of ink.

step 2

PAINT CLAY WITH DILUTED PAINT

Dilute yellow acrylic paint with water and brush it over the stamped clay. Allow the paint to settle into the impressions and let it dry.

step 3

MAKE SCRAP CLAY HANDLE

Roll a handle out of scrap clay to ⅝" (2cm) in diameter and to about 2½" (6cm) long, or to whatever dimensions are a good fit for your hands.

step 4

WRAP STAMPED CLAY AROUND HANDLE

Wrap the stamped and painted piece of clay around the handle, rolling it all the way around, and then roll the clay back and cut it precisely at the line. Finish wrapping the clay.

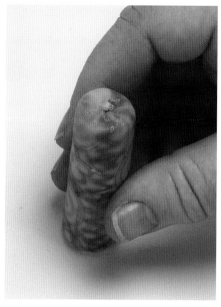

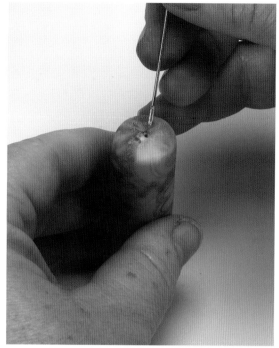

step6

INSERT NEEDLE INTO HANDLE

Insert the needle into the handle with the sharp end facing out. Bake the tool at 250°F (121°C) for 20 minutes. Let the tool cool and then rebake it at 250°F (121°C) for another 20 minutes. When the tool cools, check to make sure the needle is still secure. You may have to remove it and add a drop of Zap-A-Gap to secure it back into place.

step5

SECURE CLAY AT HANDLE ENDS

Pinch the ends of the clay closed and tamp each end on your work surface to smooth them out. Roll the edges of the ends on your work surface to round them slightly.

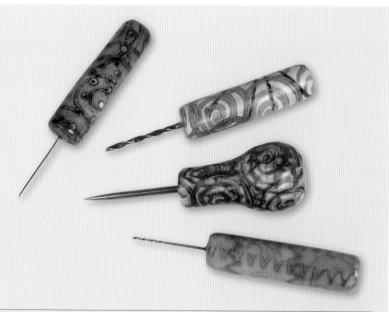

step7

APPLY LIQUID POLYCLAY AND CURE WITH HEAT GUN

Brush Liquid Polyclay onto the handle. Use the heat gun to cure the liquid polymer clay, holding the needle end of the tool with pliers if the metal gets too hot.

More Cool Tools Use small drill bits and different sizes of needles for other tools. The awl is a purchased leather awl with a wooden handle that has a veneer of clay baked onto it. Other awls and punches can be made with nails and needles of different sizes.

- dark purple Kato polymer clay
- pale cream Kato polymer clay
- Liquid Polyclay
- hair clip
- leaf rubber stamp (HERO ARTS)
- swirls stamp (JUDIKINS)
- purple inkpad (STAZON)
- re-inkers (ANCIENT PAGE)
- gold metallic acrylic paint
- purple permanent marker
- paintbrush
- craft knife
- scissors
- brayer
- small paint palette
- Zap-A-Gap

featured technique

almost metallic leafing

Gilded Leaf
Hair Clip

There is a technique in the clay kingdom (I believe that it was Tory Hughes who first showed this on polymer clay) where you burnish a sheet of gold leafing to a smooth sheet of clay. Then you roll it through the pasta machine. The clay expands, breaking the leaf into lots of little pieces. This technique with the gold acrylic paint looks similar to the leafing process. And, of course, gold paint is not as expensive as gold leaf.

Kato clay is specified for this project because it will be flexible after baking so you can shape it to the hair clip when gluing.

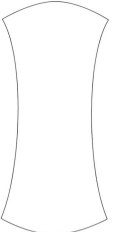

Pattern is shown at full size.

step 1

STAMP CLAY AND BRUSH ON GOLD

For the hair clip backing, roll a sheet of dark purple clay through the pasta machine at the thickest setting. Make an uninked stamped impression of swirls or any small but open design that you like. Brush gold paint onto the surface of the clay, avoiding pushing paint into the depressions of the image. Let the paint dry completely.

step 2

FLATTEN PAINTED CLAY PIECE

Flatten the painted clay piece by running it through the pasta machine or by running over it with a brayer.

step 3

CUT SHAPE FROM CLAY

Lay the template on the clay and trace around the shape with a craft knife (see pattern). Smooth the edges if necessary. Set aside.

step 4

STAMP CREAM CLAY WITH LEAF

Roll a sheet of cream clay through the pasta machine on the thickest setting. Stamp the cream clay with the leaf shape using purple ink. Cut the leaf out with a craft knife or scissors. Bake both the leaf and the purple backing at 250°F (121°C) for about seven minutes. Flatten while cooling.

step5

PAINT LEAF WITH COLORS

Mix a small amount of Liquid Polyclay with different colors of re-inkers. I'm using yellow, cobalt blue and red ink. Paint the colored Liquid Polyclay over the leaf with a small paintbrush. Bake at 250°F (121°C) for another seven minutes.

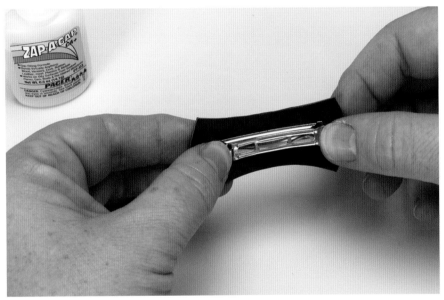

step6

ATTACH PIECES

Attach the purple swirls piece to the hair clip with Zap-A-Gap. Hold it in place for about seven seconds to secure it.

step7

FINISH HAIR CLIP

To finish, outline the leaf edges with a dark purple permanent marker. Attach the leaf to the purple backing with Zap-A-Gap.

materials

- translucent polymer clay
- scrap clay
- Liquid Polyclay
- key ring
- two seed beads
- two small glass beads
- three tiny glass dangle beads
- 20-gauge wire
- textured rubber stamps (**HERO ARTS AND JUDIKINS**)
- permanent inkpads
- permanent marker (**GALAXY**)
- thin knitting needle
- round-nose pliers
- chain-nose pliers
- wire cutters
- flush cutters
- heat gun
- wet/dry sandpaper in 320-, 400- and 600-grit
- bowl of water

featured technique

translucent stampings

Muted Mysteries
Key Ring

You can create a beautiful muted effect by stamping onto the backside of a very thin sheet of translucent polymer clay, letting the ink dry, and then covering another clay shape with the translucent clay. The base clay shows through the translucent clay, as do the stamped images. This key ring has been made with one sheet of translucent clay layered over plain scrap clay for a muted overall effect. If your base is marbled colors, then you will have added texture. You can also stamp another thin sheet and cover the first with it to create an interesting, multi-layered look. With two layers, the translucent clay will be more transparent if you bake the piece between layering. For best results, you'll need to roll the translucent sheet at the thinnest setting possible.

67

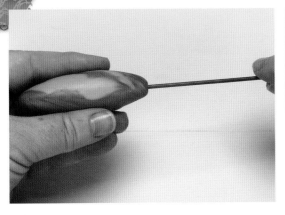

step 1

MAKE SCRAP CLAY BEAD

Roll a large, long oval bead out of scrap clay. Thread the bead onto a thin metal rod or a thin knitting needle. Set it on clay piers (see Polymer Clay Techniques, page 16) and bake at 250°F (121°C) for 30–40 minutes.

helpful **tip**

You must not touch finished (baked, sanded and polished) polymer clay with hands that have raw clay on them. It will start a reaction with the plasticizers and cause the finished clay to become dull and tacky.

step 2

STAMP TRANSLUCENT CLAY

Roll a piece of translucent clay through the pasta machine to the thinnest setting and lay it out on your work surface. Stamp all over the clay sheet with permanent ink in whatever colors you like. Let the ink dry. Highlight the stamped lines with a permanent marker, making designs as you like.

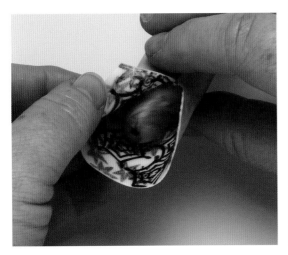

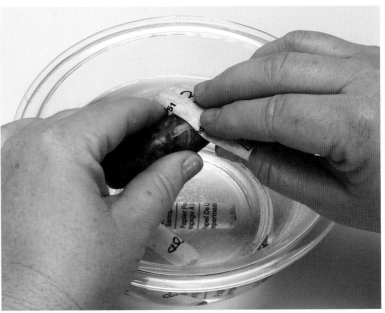

step 3

COVER SCRAP CLAY BEAD WITH TRANSLUCENT CLAY

Cover the scrap clay bead with the sheet of stamped translucent clay, keeping the decorated side facing toward the scrap clay bead. None of the design will show until after baking. Bake at 250°F (121°C) for 15 minutes. Let cool.

step 4

SAND BAKED BEAD

To smooth the surface of the baked bead, sand it with wet/dry sandpaper, beginning with 320-grit, and increasing to 400- and then to 600-grit. Wet the sandpaper and/or the baked bead as you sand.

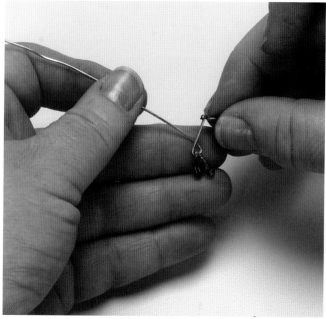

step5

BLAST BEAD WITH HEAT GUN

Blast the bead with a heat gun to bring up the shine and the translucence of the clay.

If you need to do more stamping, do so at this point. If you've added more stamping, you will want to protect it with a layer of Liquid Polyclay. Rebake the piece at 250°F (121°C) for ten minutes or cure it with a heat gun.

step6

BEND WIRE

Bend the last ½" to 1" (1cm to 3cm) of a piece of 20-gauge wire into a U shape with round-nose pliers. Slide three dangles onto the loop.

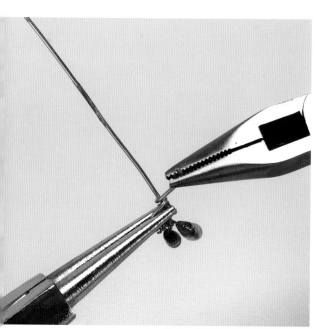

step7

MAKE A WRAPPED LOOP

Hold the loop with the round-nose pliers, grab the free end of the wire with the chain-nose pliers and wrap the tail around the loop several times. Tuck the wire end tightly into place with pliers. Then thread the long end of the wire through a glass bead.

step8

FINISH KEY RING

Thread a seed bead, a small glass bead, the clay bead, a small glass bead and then another seed bead onto the wire. Bend the wire into a U shape with round-nose pliers, then slide on the key ring. Finish by using the chain-nose pliers to wrap the wire tail around the loop to secure the key ring. Clip away any excess wire with flush cutters.

materials

dark green polymer clay

copper Kato polymer clay

box form
(I USE A LITTLE CIGAR BOX)

leafy rubber stamps (JUDIKINS)

inkpads in autumn colors
(CLEARSNAP CRAFTER'S
INKPADS)

black permanent marker

acrylic gloss varnish
(TREASURE CRYSTAL COTE)

small clay cutter in any shape

tissue blade

flex blade

heat gun

straight edge

aluminum foil

fiberfill

Zap-A-Gap

featured
technique

**elegant
elements**

Autumnal Sensibilities
Trinket Box

Delicate autumn leaves dance across copper clay as one star takes center stage pirouetting on a pretty medallion on this box. As functional art, you'll find that this type of box construction is fast and quite easy. The rim-inside-the-lid technique can be applied to any shape of box including freeform boxes or irregular shapes such as hearts, trees or any other shape you can think of. Here again, I am recommending Kato clay for the box itself because of its flexibility after baking. It will make the box less prone to breaking than if you use some of the other clays.

helpful tip

Wood may leech sap when it is baked so, to be safe, you will want to cover the wooden form with aluminum foil before adding the clay. The aluminum also makes it easier to remove the baked clay from the form.

step 1

WRAP BOX IN ALUMINUM FOIL

Wrap the box with its lid closed in aluminum foil.

step 2

CUT OUT SIDES OF BOX

Roll a piece of clay through the pasta machine at the thickest setting. Lay the clay on your work surface, and place the aluminum-covered box on top of it. Cut around the box to create a bottom and a top piece of clay. Repeat for the remaining four sides of the box, leaving a margin of about ⅟₁₆" (2mm) around each of these remaining four sides.

step 3

COVER BOX IN CLAY

Attach all of the clay pieces to the box form over the aluminum foil, securing the panels together by pinching the edges together and smoothing all of the seams.

step 4

STAMP LEAF IMAGE OVER BOX

Stamp the leaf image all over the box, overlapping and in different colors. You may use a heat gun to dry the ink more quickly so that you don't have to wait to continue with the next steps.

step5

CUT HOLES IN BOX

Use a small clay cutter to cut holes in the top center of the box. Two or three holes are enough to allow the steam to escape during baking.

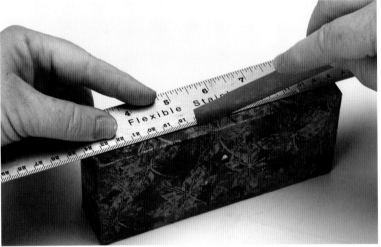

step6

CUT AROUND BOX OPENING

With a tissue blade and a straight edge, cut a line all the way around the box. This will be the separation line for the top lid and the bottom section of the box. Bake the box at 250°F (121°C) for 15 minutes and let it cool.

step7

REMOVE BAKED BOX FROM FORM

Carefully remove the baked clay lid and box from the form.

step8

BLACKEN EDGES OF BOX

Draw a black line with a permanent marker around all of the edges of the box.

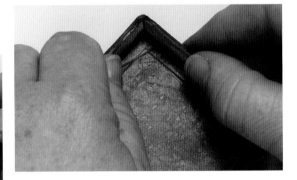

step9

COVER INSIDE EDGES OF LID

Run another sheet of clay through the pasta machine at the thickest setting. Cut strips of clay that measure about ⅜" (1cm) wide by the length of the inside of the box top. Repeat for two shorter strips that fit inside the ends of the box. Adhere these strips of clay to the inside of the box with Zap-A-Gap, mitering the corners as you go. Bake the box at 250°F (121°C) for 15 minutes.

step 10

CUT OUT LEAF-STAMPED RECTANGLE

Run a piece of copper clay through the pasta machine at a medium-thick setting. Stamp the sheet of clay all over with the leaf stamps. Cut the clay into a rectangular shape with curved ends using a flex blade.

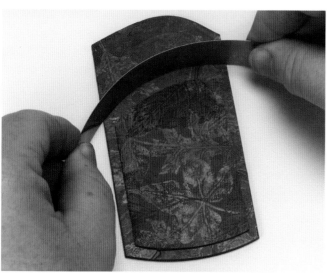

step 11

LAYER COPPER CLAY ON TOP OF GREEN

Stamp leaves all over a medium-thin sheet of dark green clay. Lay the copper sheet of clay on top of the green sheet and cut around the copper sheet, leaving about ¼" (6mm) border of green.

step 12

CREATE CLAY BORDER

Cut two very thin strips from the leftover sheet of stamped green clay and place them as borders at the top and bottom edges of the medallion. Trim the strips of clay to fit. Bake the medallion at 250°F (121°C) for 15 minutes.

step 13

ATTACH LEAF TO BOX TOP

Stamp a copper leaf and cut it out. Shape the leaf so that it looks like it has movement. Bake it on a bed of fiberfill. Coat the medallion with acrylic gloss varnish and let it dry. Use Zap-A-Gap to attach the leaf to the decorative medallion, and to attach the medallion assemblage to the top of the lid.

materials

Purse

- ½ yard sturdy fabric for liner
- ½ yard sturdy fabric for bag and handles
- assorted seed beads to coordinate with fabric
- bugle beads
- white thread
- beading needle
- scissors
- sewing machine or needle

Handles and Buttons

- translucent polymer clay
- ornamental design rubber stamps (MAGENTA)
- green, lime and Sienna re-inkers (ANCIENT PAGE)
- clear embossing ink
- paintbrush
- craft knife
- tissue blade
- heat gun
- pin vise with a small drill bit
- wet/dry sandpaper in 320-, 400- and 600-grit
- bowl of water

featured technique

imitative bakelite

Bakelite
Summer Purse

I hadn't planned to do a purse project until I discovered a great way to make what looks very much like Bakelite. I'll admit it—this was one of those serendipitous accidents. I was trying to imitate an amber-colored agate, but the clay decided that with the materials I was using, Bakelite was more in order. Try this with other colors of the Ancient Page re-inkers. It looks just as much like Bakelite if you do it in red, yellow or any other color.

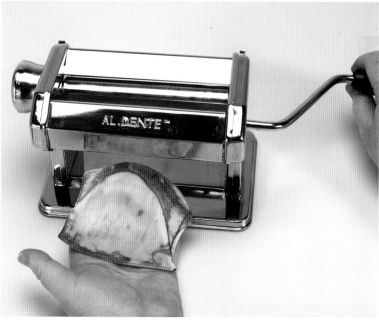

step 1

BEGIN TO MAKE BAKELITE HANDLES

Roll a sheet of translucent clay through the pasta machine at the thickest setting. Use a paintbrush to spread different colors of re-inkers onto the clay. Leave a 1" (3cm) margin of uninked clay around the edges of the sheet. Let the ink set for about 30 minutes so it begins to dry.

step 2

DISTRIBUTE COLOR EVENLY

Fold the inked sheet in half and roll the clay through the pasta machine at the thickest setting. Continue folding and rolling the clay through the pasta machine at the thickest setting until the color is fully mixed.

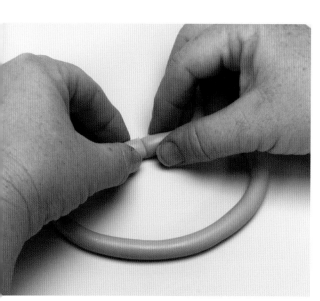

step 3

SHAPE BAKELITE HANDLES

Roll the clay into two snakes that are about 12" (30cm) long and ½" (1cm) in diameter. Cut the ends of the coil with the tissue blade and then connect them by pressing the ends together and smoothing them out. Bake the handles at 250°F (121°C) for 30 minutes.

step 4

SHINE BAKED HANDLES

Sand the handles with 320-, 400- and 600-grit wet/dry sandpaper (in that order). Blast the handles with the heat gun to bring up the shine and also to increase the depth of the translucent clay.

helpful tip

Translucent clay can quickly become very soft when you are working it. The addition of the ink will make it slightly sticky. You can zip the clay into the refrigerator for a couple minutes or you can coat stamps with clear embossing ink before you stamp into the translucent clay. The ink will act as a release agent.

step 5

MAKE BAKELITE BUTTONS

Ink another sheet of translucent clay and roll it through the pasta machine at a medium-thin setting (as in steps one and two). Stamp the clay sheet with clear embossing ink to create the buttons. Cut the button shapes out with a tissue blade and bake them at 250°F (121°C) for 15 minutes.

step 6

DRILL HOLES IN BUTTONS

Cut around the petals of the flowers with a craft knife. Drill holes into the buttons with a pin vise.

step 7

SHINE BUTTONS

When all of the buttons have been cut, blast them with the heat gun to bring up the shine.

step 8

CUT OUT FABRIC PIECES

Cut out the fabric pieces according to the following measurements: two pieces of liner fabric to 18" x 13½" (46cm x 34cm); two outside pieces of fabric to 18" x 13½" (46cm x 34cm); one handle piece of fabric to 7" x 16" (8cm x 41cm).

step 9

SEW PURSE SIDES

With right sides facing, sew two rectangular pieces of fabric together all the way around three sides, leaving the top edge open. Leave about ½" (1cm) seam all the way around. Repeat with the other two liner pieces.

step 10

BEGIN TO MAKE CORNERS

Fold the corners by grabbing both sides of the outside fabric at the corner seam and pulling them out. You'll have a triangular shape.

step 11

SEW ACROSS CORNERS

Flatten the seams and sew straight across the triangle, along an imaginary "hypotenuse."

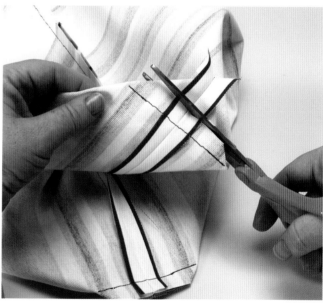

step 12

CUT OFF CORNERS

Cut off the excess corner fabric by cutting the fabric just above the seam you just sewed. Repeat steps ten through 12 for the other side of the purse and for the two corners of the liner.

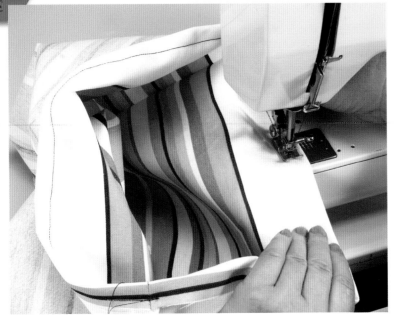

step 13

SEW HEM AT TOP OF PURSE

Sew a single-fold hem along the top of the purse and the liner, leaving a ½" (1cm) seam allowance.

step 14

REINFORCE PURSE BOTTOM AND SIDES

Turn the purse right-side out. Sew a seam about ⅟₁₆" (2mm) in from the side of the purse. Repeat for the other side. Sew a seam up each side as well. Reinforce the bottom and sides of the liner as well.

step 15

BEGIN TO MAKE FABRIC PIECE TO SUPPORT HANDLES

Fold the remaining piece of fabric in half lengthwise, with right sides facing. Sew a seam lengthwise. Turn the fabric right-side out to make a tube. Press the fabric tube, then cut it in half.

helpful **tip** If you want the bottom of the purse to be even stiffer, you can place a rectangle of plastic canvas in the bottom of the purse, between the outside and the liner.

step 16

SEW HANDLES ONTO PURSE

Fold one of the pieces of fabric from step 15 around one of the handles. Sew the ends of the fabric together about 1½" to 2" (4cm to 5cm) above the edges. Repeat for the other handle. Sew the handles to the purse liner with a seam about 2" (4cm) or so from the bottom of the handle.

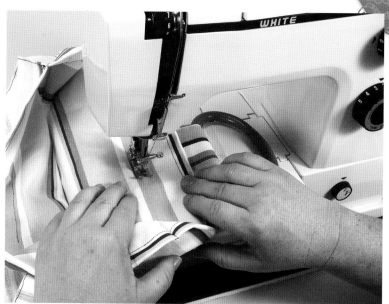

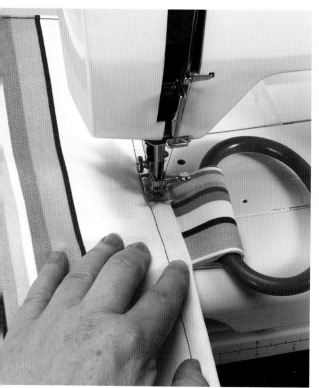

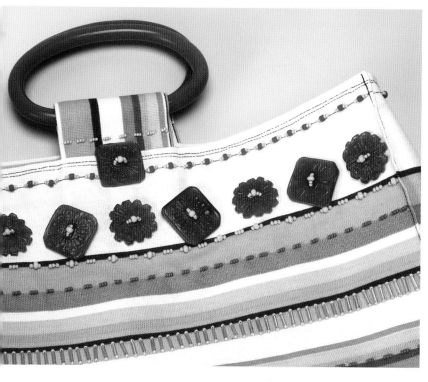

step 17

SEW IN PURSE LINER

Insert the liner into the outside shell of the purse. Sew the top edges of the purse and the liner together, leaving about a ½" (1cm) seam allowance down from the top edge. Sew another seam about ⅛" (3mm) down from the top.

step 18

SEW ON BAKELITE BUTTONS

Sew a line of buttons along the top front side of the purse by bringing the needle and thread up through one button hole, stringing on three beads, and bringing the thread back down through the second button hole.

step 19

SEW ON BEADS

Sew various seed beads and bugle beads in the colors of your choice in lines along the front side of the purse.

Home Accessories

Since polymer clay is inexpensive and oh-so-adaptable, it is a perfect medium for making home accessories. You can even hang it on your wall—check out the Polymer Paintings in this section if you don't believe me! In this chapter, you'll continue to see the never-ending possibilities for creating the perfect motif in colors and textures that suit your style. You can create checks, stripes and any other zingy pattern you can imagine when you combine rubber stamping with polymer clay. You'll be able to customize an accent piece to pick up the colors in your furniture or the design in your rug.

Need decorative plates? Walls calling for small paintings? Furniture begging for protective coasters? Polymer clay is your medium! In this section you'll find some great accent pieces for your home. There is a charger plate featuring a collage under glass, an inspirational decorative bowl for your coffee table, small colorful bowls that look like kaleidoscopes, and much more. There is a whole world of homes out there begging for your clay creations. Get busy! All of your friends are waiting for their new polymer clay home accessories!

materials

- blue polymer clay
- yellow polymer clay
- lime green polymer clay
- orange polymer clay
- peach polymer clay
- orange-yellow polymer clay
- pale aqua polymer clay
- pale cream polymer clay
- clean, clear glass plate
- fish and swirls rubber stamps **(JUDIKINS AND HERO ARTS)**
- green, bright blue, gold and silver Mica Magic inkpads **(CLEARSNAP)**
- mica powders
- gold leafing pen
- paintbrush
- pencil
- compass
- tissue blade
- scissors
- craft knife
- tiny circle cutter
- small star cutter
- rotary cutter with decorative blade
- straight edge
- piece of paper larger than plate

featured technique

collage clay under glass

Under the Sea
Collage Charger Plate

Can't you just picture a whole table set with your colorful and unique charger plates? Lustrous Mica inks, fish, swirls and patterns on this plate echo a day of tide pools, sand and summer fun. The themes and color combinations are endless—you can be as sophisticated or as playful as you like with these plates. With the sealed clay on the bottom of the dish, there is not a concern for food safety. Still, this plate is not washer friendly, so I would use it as a charger or solely as a decorative plate that is not meant for food consumption.

step1

PREPARE CLAY SHAPES

Run all of the clay colors through the pasta machine at the thinnest setting. Stamp fish onto the orange, peach and orange-yellow clay with the green and bright blue inkpads. Stamp silver swirls onto the lime green clay and punch little holes in the centers of the swirls with a clay cutter. Stamp green flowers on the pale aqua clay and punch little holes out of the petals. Stamp blue circles onto the aqua clay, punch a star shape out of the middle and cut out circles. Cut out all of the stamped images with scissors.

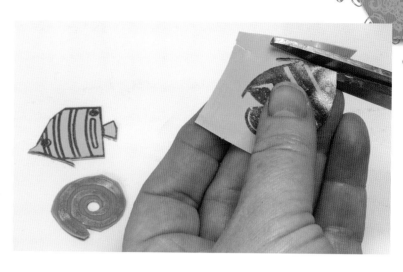

step2

COLLAGE SHAPES ONTO PLATE BOTTOM

Turn the plate over and arrange the stamped images in a collage. Firmly press the pieces down against the glass so there are no air bubbles and so that the design looks like it was printed onto one smooth slab of clay.

step4

CREATE CIRCLE TEMPLATE

Trace the glass dish onto a piece of paper and cut it out. Fold the paper circle into eighths. Unfold the circle and use a compass to draw a smaller circle in the center of the template. Cut out the template. Run the clay for the backing through the thickest setting on the pasta machine.

step3

CHECK COLLAGE DESIGN FROM FRONT OF PLATE

As you apply the stamped images, continuously check the front side to make sure the design looks the way you want it to.

step5

STAMP CLAY CIRCLE FOR BACKING

Lay the pattern for the smaller circle on a piece of cream clay and cut out the circle. Stamp the clay circle with green ink and let it dry. Apply the circle to the very center of the back of the plate.

step6

CUT REMAINING BACKING PIECES

Use the craft knife and the outer circle of the template to cut out eight more pieces for the backing. Place them on top of the collage. Here, I alternate between yellow and blue pieces of clay along the rim of the plate.

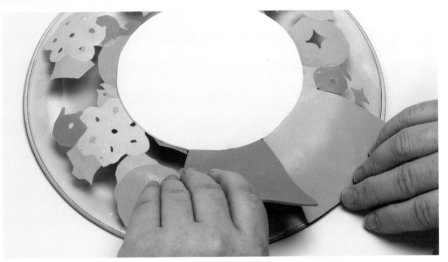

step7

DECORATE CLAY BACKING

Stamp the clay backing with uninked stamps and spread mica powders over the entire surface. Trim the edge of the clay with a rotary cutter. Bake the plate face down at 250°F (121°C) for 30 minutes.

step8

DECORATE EDGES OF PLATE

Run a gold leafing pen around the edge of the plate.

m a t e r i a l s

scrap clay or any color clay
for background

cream polymer clay

beige polymer clay

pale green polymer clay

mat board for backing

frame

flower, abstract patterns and
text rubber stamps (JUDIKINS,
STAMPOTIQUE, HERO ARTS)

purple, olive green and
pumpkin permanent inkpads
(STAZON)

metallic Mica Magic inkpad
(CLEARSNAP)

purple acrylic paint

craft knife

small star clay cutter

two sizes of circle clay cutters

brayer

decorative-edge rotary cutter

foam paintbrush

straight edge

wide mosaic double-stick tape
(JUDIKINS)

cutting mat

glue

featured
technique

**"painting"
with clay**

Polymer
Painting

Running random mosaics of scrap clay through the pasta machine creates the most
beautiful and fluid patterns that, for me, recall layered brushstrokes of paint. Always
interesting, the flattened clay looked like little paintings, so I thought, "Why not?" Why
not stamp, cut out and add a few elements to the already cool background clay and make
a painting? These collaged sheets look as great on cards as they do mounted and framed
for wall art. The pages that follow give you the steps to create the specific painting shown
here, but feel free to have fun creating your own artistic designs.

Metallic and pearlized polymer clays are made with mica dust. You can make your own shiny clays by adding mica powder to any colored clay. For instance, if you want a pale gold clay, you can add white clay to the gold clay. It will then lose some of its metallic luster. To refuel the sheen, add pale gold mica powder to the clay mix. You can do this with any clay color and any mica powder.

step 1

PREPARE "CANVAS"

Roll a sheet of clay at the thickest setting on the pasta machine to create your canvas. You may use scrap clay, and your sheet may be smooth or marbled in coloration. Stamp the clay sheet with a metallic color of Mica Magic that complements the background color you choose.

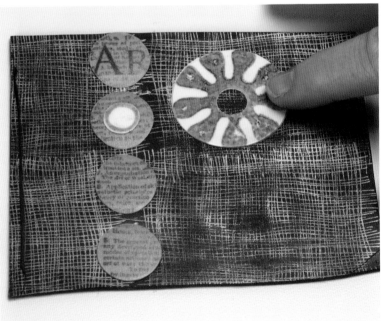

step 2

CUT FOUR CIRCLES FROM STAMPED CLAY SHEET

Stamp a small sheet of medium-thin beige clay with a text stamp using olive green ink. Use a circle cutter to cut four circles from the stamped clay.

step 3

POSITION CLAY CUT-OUTS ON CANVAS

Stamp a pop flower onto thin cream clay using purple ink. Cut a circle around the flower with a clay cutter or a craft knife. Position the circles from step two and the flower on the stamped canvas.

step4

CUT OUT DECORATIVE ELEMENTS

Load a foam brush with purple acrylic paint and ink a stamp with it. Stamp the image onto pale green clay that has been run through the pasta machine at a thin setting. Cut the sheet of green clay into strips with a decorative-edge rotary cutter.

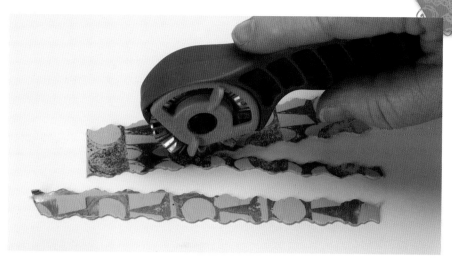

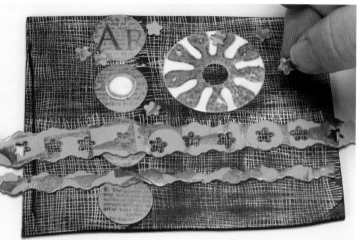

step5

POSITION CLAY STRIPS ON CANVAS

Use the star clay cutter to punch little stars out of the strips. Place the stars and the strips onto the canvas.

step6

BRAYER ALL ELEMENTS TO BACKGROUND

Adhere all of the clay components to the background by brayering over them with a clay roller. Stamp stars onto the canvas with pumpkin-colored ink.

helpful *tip*

If you're using a dark clay background, stamp with lighter color inks that will show up more clearly. If using a light clay background, stamp with darker ink for more contrast.

step7

BLEND PAINTING

Roll the canvas through the pasta machine at the thickest setting. Turn the pasta machine to the next thinnest setting, rotate the canvas one quarter turn and run it through again. Turn the pasta machine to the next thinnest setting and run it through again in the same direction. Bake at 250°F (121°C) for 15 minutes. Flatten the piece while it's cooling.

step8

CUT PAINTING TO FIT MAT

Lay your design on a cutting mat. Align the piece on the mat and cut along the edges with a craft knife. Cut the "canvas" into a rectangular shape that fits onto your mat with a wide margin. The size of my canvas is 5½" x 5" (14cm x 13cm).

step9

ADHERE PAINTING TO MAT BOARD

Apply double-stick tape to the back of the polymer clay piece and adhere it to the mat board. Cut a coordinating mat board frame and glue it to the base. You may add additional decorative elements to the frame around the painting, if you wish.

Another Polymer Painting Your base clay "canvas" can be any color or texture. Here is a variation with a light background rather than dark, as shown in the main project. Consider making smaller paintings to go onto cards or book fronts. How about tiny polymer paintings to be used in jewelry? Wouldn't it look fabulous to cut a tiny oval piece of clay painting and nestle it into a silver setting? You could make several and attach them in different ways to form a beautifully creative and unique bracelet.

assorted colors of polymer clay

set of plain cork coasters

four 2" (5cm) ball-ended wooden pegs

four 1" (3cm) round wooden or polymer beads with a ¼" (6mm) hole and flat bottom

text rubber stamps (STAMPOTIQUE AND JUDIKINS)

permanent inkpads (LIKE STAZON AND MICA MAGIC)

gold Krylon marker

scissors

pin vise with ¼" (6mm) drill bit

wide mosaic tape (JUDIKINS)

white glue

featured technique

"painting" with clay

Coasters and
Caddy Set

How about coasters as another small canvas opportunity? With stamped words of encouragement or clever verses, your coasters can be entertaining as well as functional furniture protection. To hold the set together when not in use, you will want to make a quick coaster caddy. Start these coasters with a selection of polymer clay paintings as outlined in the previous project. Then follow the step-outs to complete the set.

step1

MAKE POLYMER PAINTINGS

Make several polymer paintings, one for each coaster, as shown in the Polymer Painting project (page 85). Bake the sheets at 250°F (121°C) for 15 minutes. Flatten them as they cool.

step2

CUT OUT COASTER SHAPES

Trace a cork coaster onto each polymer painting and use scissors to cut the coaster shapes out. Cut out as many coasters as you'd like in your set plus an additional coaster to create the bottom of the caddy.

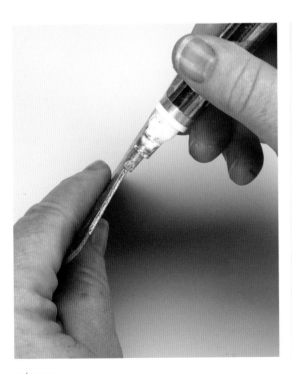

step3

COLOR COASTER EDGES GOLD

Color the edges of the coasters with gold paint pen.

step4

ADD STAMPED DECORATION TO COASTERS

Use permanent ink to over-stamp a sentiment or more decoration onto the baked clay artwork.

step5

ADHERE CLAY TO CORK BACKING

Glue the artwork to the cork backing with wide mosaic tape.

step6

MAKE COASTER CADDY

Use a ¼" (6mm) pin vise to make a hole in each corner of one of the coasters.

step7

COLOR CADDY COMPONENTS GOLD

Color the wooden beads and the dowel pieces with gold paint pen.

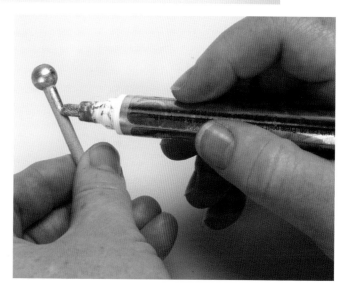

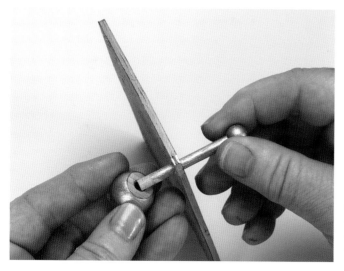

step8

CREATE CADDY LEGS

Insert the wooden peg through one hole and glue the big bead with the flat bottom to the other end of the peg with white glue. Repeat for the other three legs of the coaster caddy.

step9

FINISH COASTER SET

Stack the coasters into the caddy by angling them diagonally between the caddy legs.

materials

turquoise polymer clay

Liquid Polyclay

glass container

wavy lines rubber stamp
for border (STAMPOTIQUE)

swirl stamp (HERO ARTS)

copper acrylic paint

gold acrylic paint

clear gloss (KRYLON)

paintbrush

craft knife

tissue blade

soft cloth

Zap-A-Gap

featured
technique

**simply
impressive**

Dome-Top
Glass Container

A small glass votive candle holder can be made into a cute container for jewels and other precious belongings, or it can be, well…a small glass votive candle holder. But, now it has a cool lid that is also a candle-flame snuffer. I've used metallic acrylic paint on this vessel in a dimensional version of the almost metallic leafing used in the Gilded Leaf Hair Clip on page 64. This project would also look great if you brushed a mica powder coating onto the raw clay, baked it and then sealed it with a gloss coat. For another variation, try inking the rubber stamp with a permanent inkpad and then stamping into the clay.

step2

ADHERE CLAY CIRCLE TO BOTTOM OF CONTAINER

Spread Liquid Polyclay onto the bottom of the glass and center the glass onto the disk of clay. Press down gently. Bake the piece at 250°F (121°C) for 15 minutes and set aside to cool.

step3

STAMP CLAY BORDERS

Roll a piece of turquoise clay through the pasta machine at a medium-thick setting. Stamp the three uninked border designs onto the clay and cut them apart with a clay blade. Bake the borders at 250°F (121°C) for ten minutes.

step1

CREATE CLAY TOP AND BOTTOM

Roll turquoise clay through the pasta machine at the thickest setting and divide it into two pieces. Place the glass container on one piece of clay and cut around it, leaving a ⅛" (3mm) border. Repeat with the other piece of turquoise clay. Set aside one circle for the lid.

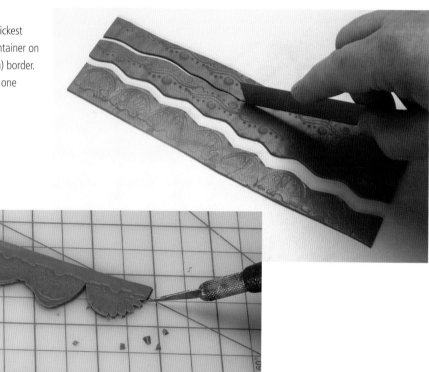

step4

CUT OUT BORDERS

Cut the baked borders out close to the stamp line and make a decorative design at the edge using a craft knife.

step5

ADHERE BORDERS TO CLAY BASE

Adhere the wider border to the bottom edge of the glass, staying on top of the extended disk shape. Glue it into place with Zap-A-Gap. Repeat with the smaller border, overlapping the first border slightly.

step 6

MAKE CLAY ROPE

Cut two long, thin strips of clay from a piece of clay that has been run through the pasta machine at a medium-thin setting. Twist the two pieces of clay together to form a "rope." Bake the twisted clay at 250°F (121°C) for 15 minutes and let it cool.

step 7

ADHERE CLAY ROPE TO BOTTOM BORDER

Glue the "rope" to the bottom of the vessel with Zap-A-Gap, overlapping both the bottom disk and the bottom border. Allow the glue to dry.

step 8

MAKE CLAY LID FOR CONTAINER

Bake the circle of clay for the lid. Roll a small piece of turquoise clay through the pasta machine at the thickest setting and cut out a ¼" (6mm) wide strip of clay that is about 1" (3cm) longer than the circumference of the baked lid. Brush the edges of the lid with liquid polymer clay and press the strip of clay onto the inside edge of the lid. Bake the lid at 250°F (121°C) for 15 minutes and let it cool.

step 9

BEGIN TO CREATE CLAY DOME

Roll a large ball of turquoise clay to a size that just fits inside the glass container. If you like, you can use scrap clay to make the ball and then cover it with a thin sheet of colored clay.

step 10

CUT CLAY BALL IN HALF

Cut the clay ball in half with a tissue blade

step 11

ADHERE DOME TO CLAY LID

Spread Liquid Polyclay onto the lid and press the dome to the lid.

step 12

SHAPE DOME

Use your hands to flatten the dome and smooth it, shaping it so that it reaches the edges.

step 13

STAMP DOME

Stamp uninked swirl images onto the dome. Bake it at 250°F (121°C) for 15 minutes.

step 14

COVER SEAM ON LID

Use Zap-A-Gap to adhere one of the thinner borders from step four around the lid's rim. Use a portion of the coiled rope to cover the seam between the rim and the dome, using Zap-A-Gap to adhere it.

step 15

FINISH DOME

Roll a piece of clay through the pasta machine at the thickest setting and stamp a swirl onto it with the uninked stamp. Cut around a single swirl with a craft knife. Bake the swirl at 250°F (121°C) for ten minutes. Adhere it to the top of the dome on the lid with Zap-A-Gap.

step 16

PAINT CLAY TO FINISH CONTAINER

Coat the clay with copper acrylic paint. Rub off the top layer of paint with a soft cloth, leaving the paint only down in the stamped impressions. Follow up with a light coat of gold acrylic paint in some spots to let some gold and copper show. Coat the clay with a clear gloss, if desired.

materials

scrap clay

cadmium red polymer clay

purple polymer clay

cadmium yellow polymer clay

big dots rubber stamp
(STAMPOTIQUE)

small dots rubber stamp
(HERO ARTS)

yellow and Henna inkpads
(ANCIENT PAGE)

pumpkin inkpad (STAZON)

white inkpad (CRAFTER'S INK)

frosted white inkpad
(CRAFTER'S INK)

yellow permanent marker
(GALAXY)

white permanent marker
(GALAXY)

clear gloss varnish spray
(KRYLON)

2" (5cm) diameter wooden ball

craft knife

brayer

tissue blade

wet/dry sandpaper in
320-, 400- and 600-grit

small piece of fiberfill

bowl of water

Zap-A-Gap

featured
technique

**simply
impressive**

Dottie
Sculpture

A colorful curiosity is the name of this game. The first idea was that this would be an excellent sculpture all by itself, but as I was making it, I thought that it would be really cool to make a whole forest of these sculptures in different shapes, colors and sizes and then use them to display small items like art glass beads.

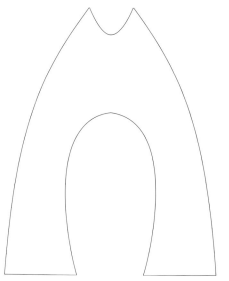

Enlarge pattern to 143% to bring to full size.

step1

MAKE "LEGS"

Roll two sheets of clay to the thickest setting on the pasta machine using new clay or scrap clay (any kind of filler clay). Stack the two sheets and brayer them together. Use the pattern provided to cut a "leg" shape out of paper to create a template. Lay the pattern on top of the layered clay and cut it out with a craft knife. Repeat for a second "leg." Bake the legs at 250°F (121°C) for 20 minutes.

step2

COVER LEGS WITH PURPLE AND YEL-LOW CLAY

Roll small amounts of purple and yellow clay to the thinnest setting on the pasta machine. Cover the "legs" with the two colors of clay. Bake the covered legs at 250°F (121°C) for 15 minutes.

step3

SAND BAKED LEGS

Use wet/dry sandpaper and water to sand the legs smooth. Start with 320-grit sandpaper, move to 400-grit and finish with 600-grit. Moisten the baked piece and/or the sandpaper as you work.

step4

STAMP LEGS

Use pumpkin-colored ink to stamp onto the yellow clay and frosted white ink to stamp small white dots onto the purple clay. Use a heat gun to dry the ink.

step5

DECORATE INSIDE EDGES OF LEGS

Use permanent markers to draw lines and dots on the inside edges of the legs, if you wish.

step6

SPRAY LEGS WITH CLEAR GLOSS VARNISH

Spray the legs with clear gloss varnish to preserve the ink.

step7

ADHERE LEGS TOGETHER TO CREATE STAND

Put a drop of Zap-A-Gap onto each point of one leg. Press the legs together so that they will stand up on their own.

step8

BEGIN TO MAKE BOWL

To create the bowl, wrap one half of a wooden ball with red clay rolled through the pasta machine at the thickest setting. Trim away the excess clay with a tissue blade. Bake the bowl on a bed of fiberfill at 250°F (121°C) for ten minutes.

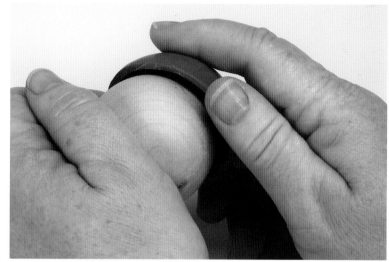

step9

PEEL BOWL SHAPE FROM WOODEN BALL

While the clay is still slightly warm and pliable, carefully peel the bowl shape off of the wooden ball form.

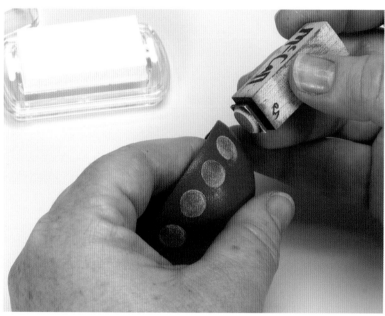

step10

STAMP BOWL

Stamp dots onto the outside rim of the bowl with white ink and let it dry. Repeat for a more opaque white and let dry.

step11

FINISH DECORATING BOWL

Over-stamp the white dots with yellow ink. Let it dry. Use a yellow permanent marker to make little dots all around the yellow dots on the bowl's rim. Let dry. Draw little white stripes on the top rim of the bowl with a white permanent marker. Let dry.

step12

FINISH SCULPTURE

Spray the bowl with a gloss coat and let it dry. Attach the bowl on top of the legs with a couple drops of Zap-A-Gap.

materials

- turquoise polymer clay
- orange polymer clay
- purple polymer clay
- celadon (pale green) polymer clay
- small glass bowl
- snowflake, medallion, text and other geometric shape rubber stamps (JUDIKINS AND STAMPER'S ANONYMOUS)
- purple and pumpkin inkpads (STAZON)
- white acrylic paint
- gloss varnish
- craft knife
- assorted clay cutters
- foam brush

featured technique

acrylic stampings

Kaleidoscope
Bowls

Colorful bowls made of intricately patterned canes have always captivated me, whether made of glass or clay. Those fascinating bowls are what led to this design concept. I used both acrylic paint and ink to stamp the images that make up this kaleidoscopic bowl. The results are both old-world and contemporary and make an exciting addition to any décor.

step 1

STAMP TURQUOISE CLAY WITH WHITE PAINT

Prepare all clay by running in through the thickest setting on the pasta machine. Use a foam brush to apply white acrylic paint to your round medallion stamp and apply the stamp to four squares of unbaked turquoise clay.

step 3

STAMP ORANGE CLAY WITH PURPLE INK

Use purple ink to stamp eight smaller medallions onto orange clay.

step 2

STAMP PURPLE CLAY WITH WHITE PAINT

Apply white paint to the snowflake stamp and stamp the image onto seven squares of purple clay.

step 4

STAMP GREEN CLAY

Roll a piece of celadon clay through the pasta machine at a medium-thin setting to a size that accommodates the text stamp. Stamp the clay with orange ink. Cut out four box-like shapes from the celadon clay using a clay cutter.

step5

PUNCH HOLES IN SNOWFLAKE

Use a craft knife to cut around one large snowflake image. Use a little clay cutter to punch a hole in the middle of the cut-out snowflake.

step6

PLACE PURPLE SNOWFLAKE IN BOWL

Press the purple snowflake down into the bottom center of the bowl.

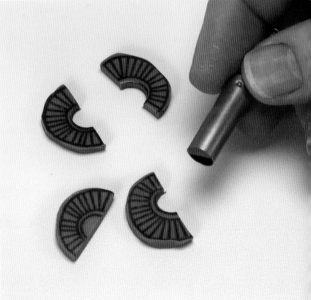

step7

CUT OUT TWO ORANGE MEDALLIONS

Cut out two orange medallions with a craft knife.

step8

MAKE ORANGE ARCHES

Slice two orange medallions in half with a craft knife. Use a clay cutter to remove the centers.

step9

PLACE ARCHES IN BOWL

Place four medallion halves against each side of the central snowflake in the bowl.

step10

PLACE TURQUOISE ARCHES

Cut around the two larger turquoise medallions with a clay blade and punch a hole in the center of each one with a clay cutter. Cut the medallions in half and place the halves around the orange halves, pressing the clay pieces together to adhere them.

step11

PUNCH OUT FLOWERS

Use a flower-shaped clay cutter to punch out eight little flowers from the stamped orange clay.

step12

PRESS FLOWERS INTO TURQUOISE ARCHES

Press the flowers into the arches of the turquoise medallions.

step 13

CUT SNOWFLAKES INTO WEDGES

Cut around the remaining four snowflakes with a craft knife. Punch out the centers of four snowflakes with a circle clay cutter. Divide the remaining snowflakes into wedges.

step 14

CUT OUT ALL PIECES

Cut out the remaining stamped pieces of clay and continue to build the bowl upward in a pattern that you like.

step 16

BAKE PIECE AND REMOVE FROM BOWL FORM

Bake the piece still adhered to the bowl at 250°F (121°C) for 15 minutes. Allow the bowl to cool and then peel the clay gently from the glass bowl. You may stamp the bottom with a text stamp in white acrylic paint and then coat it with a gloss varnish if you wish.

step 15

PLACE THE FINAL PIECES INTO THE BOWL

Finish positioning all of the clay pieces in the bottom of the bowl.

materials

pink Premo! polymer clay

white Kato polymer clay

Liquid Polyclay

set of brass wind chimes

fishing wire

18-gauge brass-colored wire

heart rubber stamps
(HERO ARTS)

black inkpad **(STAZON)**

baby blue Mica Magic inkpad
(CLEARSNAP)

colored pencils

paintbrush

craft knife

1¼" (3cm) circle cutter

tissue blade

plastic clay shaper

scissors

round-nose pliers

wire cutters

heat gun

pin vise with very small drill bit
**(A LITTLE LARGER THAN THE
FISHING WIRE)**

sheet of white copy paper
(20 BOND OR EQUALLY THIN)

light box

fiberfill

featured
technique

**colored
pencil
transfer**

Chiming
Hearts

There are many, many rubber stamps perfect for the colored pencil technique used in this project, or you could also make exciting wind chimes with any of the techniques described throughout this book. After the clay is creatively surfaced, you can shape the separate weights into really cool shapes, too. You know that phrase "limited only by your imagination?" Well, it's really true for this project. Think about adding bead and wirework to your clay, or wrap pretty beach glass or stones and hang them as part of the wind chimes. Go ahead—bring out the funk to truly make this wind chime music to your ears and eyes.

step1

STAMP HEARTS ONTO WHITE CLAY

Condition and roll out a very thin slab of white clay to the thinnest setting on the pasta machine. Stamp four hearts onto the white clay with black ink.

step2

MAKE COLORED HEART TRANSFERS

Stamp the same four hearts onto white copy paper with black ink. Flip the paper over and color the backside of the images with colored pencils. If the outline of the heart is not clear enough, use a light box. Cut out the paper hearts.

Enlarge pattern 200% to bring to full size.

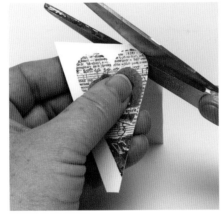

helpful **tip**   I use black StazOn ink for this project because it is a solvent ink and seeps into the copy paper a bit more than regular dye inks. That way I can see the image from the backside of the paper even without a light box. A light box definitely makes coloring easier, though.

step3

CUT OUT BAKED HEARTS

Burnish the paper hearts onto the unbaked white clay with your fingers, making sure to align them precisely over the stamped hearts on the clay. Bake the hearts at 250°F (121°C) for seven minutes and flatten to cool. Peel away the paper to reveal a matte colored image. Use scissors to cut two hearts along the stamp line and cut two hearts about 1/8" (6mm) inside the line. This will create two smaller hearts for the bottom medallion.

step4

MAKE HEARTS WITH BORDERS

To create the pink border for the top medallion, roll a slab of clay at the thickest setting on the pasta machine. Place the stamped and colored hearts on top of the pink clay and trace around them, leaving a 3/8" (1cm) border all around them. Cut out the hearts with a craft knife. Stamp the hearts with a graphic stamp and the baby blue Mica Magic ink.

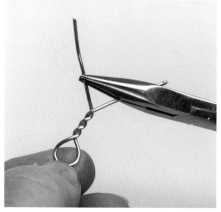

step6

TWIST ENDS OF HANGER

Twist the ends together to form a neck about ⅜" (1cm) long. Curl the ends of the wire legs that will "grab" the clay.

step5

BEGIN TO MAKE WIRE HANGER

Cut a 3" (8cm) length of 18-gauge brass wire. Center the wire over the round-nose pliers and push down to start shaping the hanger. The wire will look like a hairpin. Push the wire around the pliers so that the two ends cross and twist.

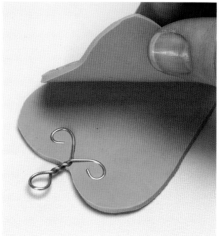

step7

SECURE HANGER

Sandwich the wire hanger in between the two pink hearts with their backsides facing each other.

step8

SMOOTH OUT HEART EDGES

Use a clay shaper to smooth the pink heart and to give a slight beveled look to the edges.

step9

APPLY LIQUID POLYCLAY TO HEART

Spread a layer of Liquid Polyclay all over one side of the pink heart and attach the white heart. Brush Liquid Polyclay over the white heart as well. Bake the heart on a sheet of polyfill at 250°F (121°C) for ten minutes. Flatten to cool. Repeat for the other side of the pink heart.

helpful **tip** Some rubber stamp companies absolutely forbid any type of mechanical reproduction of their images. No matter if you paid good money for their rubber stamps—they need to protect their artwork and their catalogs from unscrupulous people. Many rubber stamp companies are more lenient. Check the copyright statements in the catalogs, go online or call the stamp companies directly to be sure that it is OK to use their stamps for this technique.

step 10

MAKE PINK AND WHITE STRIPES

Roll a small piece of white clay and a small piece of pink clay
through the pasta machine at the thickest setting. Stack the two
pieces of clay and run them through the pasta machine together.
Then cut the stack in half and stack one half on top of the other.
Run the stack through the pasta machine again. Repeat until
you have stripes that are the width that you want on the border.

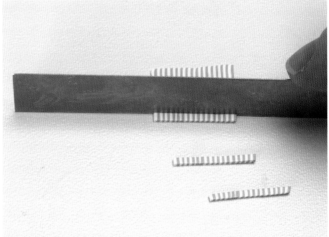

step 11

FINISH STRIPES

Cut and stack the stripes of clay until the stack is about 1" (3cm)
thick. Cut thin slices off of the stack with a tissue blade.

step 12

CUT SLICES INTO NARROW STRIPS

Cut each pink-and-white striped slice into a narrow strip with
the tissue blade.

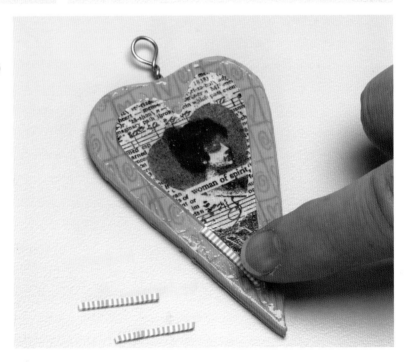

helpful
tip

Don't worry about the matte
appearance of the baked and
transferred colored pencil on
the white clay. As soon as you
gloss coat it, the color will brighten and come
back to life.

step 13

ADHERE PINK AND WHITE BORDERS

Position the pink and white strips along the edges of the white hearts and the outside edge
of the pink heart. Coat them with Liquid Polyclay and bake at 250°F (121°C) for about five
minutes more.

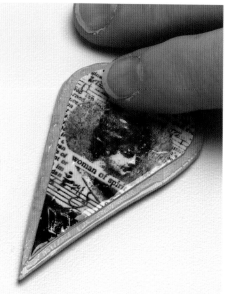

step 14

CREATE SMALLER MEDALLION

For the smaller medallion, roll a slab of pink clay through the pasta machine at a no. 2 setting. Trace the heart so that it is only about ⅛" (6mm) larger than the white heart. Stamp both the front and back of the heart with the baby blue Mica Magic ink. Let it dry or set the ink with a heat gun. Brush Liquid Polyclay over the pink heart and adhere a white heart to its center. Brush more Liquid Polyclay over the white heart. Bake the heart at 250°F (121°C) for 15 minutes and flatten to cool. Repeat on the backside of the heart.

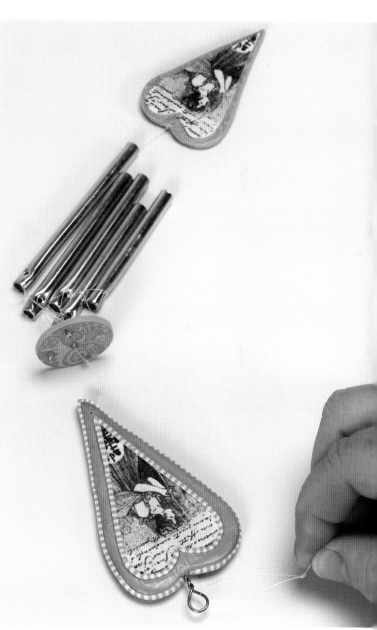

step 15

MAKE CIRCLE COMPONENT AND DRILL HOLES

Roll pink clay through the pasta machine at the thickest setting and cut out a 1¼" (3cm) circle. Stamp both sides of the circle with baby blue Mica Magic inkpad. Dry the ink with a heat gun and brush Liquid Polyclay over the top side of the circle. Bake it at 250°F (121°C) for seven minutes and flatten it as it cools. Drill one hole into the center of the circle and drill four equally spaced holes around the edge of the circle with the pin vise. Drill a hole at the bottom of the large heart medallion and one at the top of the small heart medallion as well.

step 16

CONNECT ALL PIECES WITH FISHING WIRE

String wire through all of the wind chime pieces and tie knots to secure them together. See the diagram (page 106) for the assembly sequence.

- polymer clay in a variety of complementary colors
- scrap polymer clay
- Liquid Polyclay
- Liquid Sculpey
- brass candle cup
- 10-gauge wire
- ribbon border stamps **(HERO ARTS)**
- permanent inkpads in complementary colors **(LIKE MICA MAGIC OR STAZON)**
- mica powders in complementary colors
- oil paints
- permanent marker
- tissue blade
- clay blade
- skewer
- acrylic block
- wire cutters
- heat gun
- small squeeze bottle with fine tip
- pin vise with small drill bit
- Zap-A-Gap

featured technique

lampwork elements

Lampwork
Candlestick Holder

I love the look of lampwork beads, and this is one fascinating way to make them! When I saw Judy Belcher make her small imitative beads on the *Carol Duvall Show*, I was blown away with the possibilities. I've found a couple secrets here, so read on for my own twists on Judy's process.

step 1

ROLL AND COVER FIRST BEAD

Roll a bead out of scrap clay to about 1¼" (3cm) in diameter and cover it with a sheet of fresh clay that has been run through the pasta machine at a medium-thin setting (see Polymer Clay Techniques, page 14).

step 2

SHAPE BEAD

Ink a rubber stamp with Mica Magic or any permanent ink and stamp all sides of the oval-shaped bead, but leave the top and bottom unstamped. Set the round bead on your work surface and flatten the top and bottom with the acrylic block. Bake the bead at 250°F (121°C) for one hour.

step 3

MIX COLORANT

Drill a hole through the center of the bead and thread it onto a skewer and set it aside. Fill a small squeeze bottle with a fine tip with one half Liquid Polyclay and one half Liquid Sculpey. Mix a little mica powder and a little dab of oil paint similar in color to the mica powder into the liquid clay.

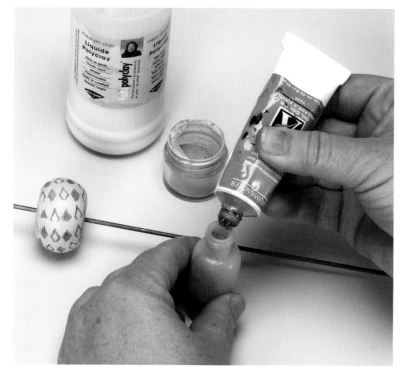

step4

ADD COLOR TO BEAD

Heat the bead with a heat gun. While the bead is hot, squeeze the liquid clay colorant mixture onto it, highlighting the stamped image. Add a few dots of liquid clay to other areas of the bead as well.

helpful **tip** You can rebake these beads in the oven, but they will not come out nearly as shiny as when coated with Liquid Polyclay and blasted with your heat gun. You will know when the color is cured because the sparkles from the mica powder will show up and the Liquid Polylclay mixture will be clear and shiny with no milkiness. You can add little dots of color onto already painted surfaces to build dimensional layers, too!

step5

HEAT BEAD

Continue to heat the bead and add color. Cure the liquid clay colorant mixture with a heat gun as you go so that the color does not run. Repeat with other colors of liquid clay colorant if desired.

step6

CREATE OTHER BEADS

Make several other beads in the same manner but in different shapes and sizes. The candlestick holder I made consists of beads of the following dimensions: 1½" (4cm) cube, 1¾" (4cm) sphere, 1¼" (3cm) cube, 1½" (4cm) sphere. Coat the cooled beads with Liquid Polyclay and bake them in the oven to cure at 250°F (121°C) for ten minutes. After the beads are baked, blast them with the heat gun to really bring up the shine. Let them cool completely before handling.

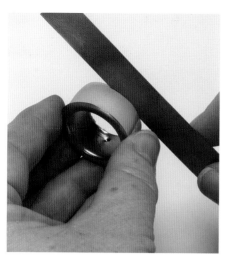

step 7

CREATE CANDLE CUP

Mold a strip of clay around the neck of a brass candle cup. Trim away the excess clay with a tissue blade. Bake the candle cup at 250°F (121°C) for ten minutes. Decorate the candle cup as you decorated the beads. Blast it with the heat gun as you go.

step 8

STACK BEADS

Stack all of the beads onto a piece of 10-gauge wire. Mark the wire with a permanent marker flush to the top of the top bead. Cut the wire to the correct size. Put Zap-A-Gap on the top 1" (3cm) of the wire, and slide on the bottom bead. Put Zap-A-Gap on the next 1" (3cm) of wire and on top of the first bead, and slide the second bead into place. Continue in this manner until you reach the candle cup.

Lampwork Beads **This process looks great on darker colors, too. Of course, my favorite is on small beads and jewelry. Ummm...did I mention that I really like making polymer jewelry?**

step 9

GLUE ON CANDLE CUP

Adhere the candle cup to the top of the stacked beads with a couple drops of Zap-A-Gap.

- black polymer clay
- grey polymer clay
- pale gold polymer clay
- small clock working
- clock hands
- assorted beads
- 10-gauge wire
- 18-gauge wire
- abstract shapes rubber stamps **(HERO ARTS, JUDIKINS AND STAMP OASIS)**
- red, green and gold mica powders
- brown and gold embossing powders
- clock face template **(OPTIONAL)**
- compass
- craft knife
- tissue blade
- ¾" (2cm) hole cutter **(OR BIG ENOUGH TO ACCOMMODATE NUT ON FRONT OF CLOCK MECHANISM)**
- brayer
- soft brush
- pen or pencil
- round-nose pliers
- needle-nose pliers
- wire cutters
- drill bit to accommodate wires
- Zap-A-Gap

featured technique

imitative raku

Timely
Tiles Clock

Look out! It's a Raku Return! Silky mica powders blend with bronze embossing powders to give a fired Raku look to these little tiles. The sleek retro design, complete with radiating spokes, contrasts nicely with the earthiness of the beaded tiles. Just about any stamp with an open design will work on the tiles. Be sure to bake extra tiles/beads for your other projects at the same time.

step 1

MAKE AND STAMP CLAY SQUARES

Stack four pieces of black clay run through the pasta machine at the thickest setting, and adhere them together by running over the stack with a brayer. Cut the stack of clay to about a 1" (3cm) width. Use a clay blade to cut the stacked strip of clay into 12 1" (3cm) squares. Squeeze each square with your fingers to soften the edges so that the squares have slightly irregular sides. Use four different uninked stamps to make impressions in each square. In this instance, I wanted the tiles to have an irregular look to them. However, if you want your tiles to be even, use a Marxit tool for incremental measurements.

helpful **tips**

Sometimes you will want to stamp both sides of the tiles. So as not to smash one side when you are stamping the other, place a skewered bead onto one stamp that is face up and press another stamp, face down, into the unbaked clay, making an impression in the clay on both sides at the same time.

I have recently perfected my new iron embossing powders from JudiKins. With inclusions that give the melted powder an old pitted texture, the powders make the clay look like you really did just dig it out of the fire pit. You must try the new powder on your Raku creations.

step 2

BRUSH MICA POWDERS ONTO SQUARES

Brush mica powders onto the stamped squares, coating the edges of the squares as well.

step3

SPRINKLE ON EMBOSSING POWDER

Sprinkle brown embossing powder over the tiles. Use your fingers to brush the powder into the stamped impression. Also sprinkle a little gold powder over the clay. Bake the clay at 250°F (121°C) for 30 minutes.

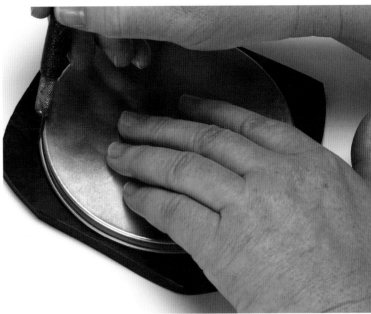

step4

MAKE CLOCK FACE

Roll three pieces of black clay through the pasta machine at the thickest setting and stack them on top of each other. Use a template or a round object that is the size of the clock face you'd like to have (mine is about 4½" [11cm]), lay it on top of the stacked clay and cut around it with a craft knife.

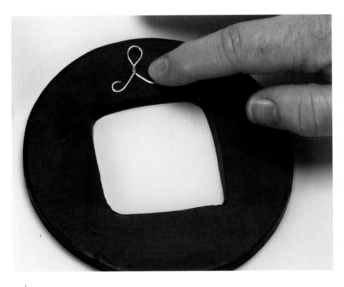

step5

MAKE HANGER

Lay the clock working on the center of the clock face, and cut out a slot in the clay to accommodate it. With the round-nose pliers, bend a 2½" (6cm) piece of 18-gauge wire into a U shaped hanger and cross the wire legs. Curl the ends of the wires to help them grip the clay. Attach the hanger to the upper backside of the clock face by pressing the little legs into the unbaked clay.

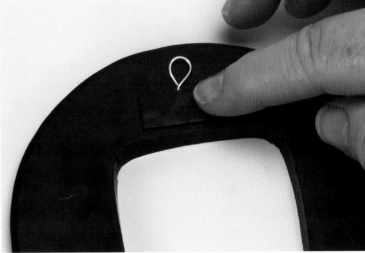

step6

SECURE HANGER

Cut a small rectangle out of a thin piece of black clay and cover the legs of the wire hanger with it, pressing down gently to adhere it.

step 7

DECORATE CLOCK FACE

Stamp the front of the clock face all over with an uninked stamp. Brush mica powders all over the clock face and on the edges of the clock. Sprinkle brown and gold embossing powders over the mica powders, using your fingers to brush the powders into the impressions. Bake the clay at 250°F (121°C) for 30 minutes. Do not flatten the clay after it is baked.

helpful **tip**

I rarely make a hole through my clay pieces before they are baked. I prefer drilling into the clay afterward so I can avoid distortion and fingerprints on the unbaked clay. I also make extra pieces while I am at it. Then I put them away until I know what I want to make with them. I don't want to be limited with a baked piece of clay that already has a hole in it at the exact spot that I do not need that hole to be.

step 8

DRILL HOLES IN TILES

Use wire cutters to cut 12 3½" (9cm) lengths of 10-gauge wire. Use the drill bit to make a hole through each of the tiles.

step 9

SECURE TILES ON WIRE SPOKES

Slide a bead, a tile and another bead onto a wire length. Move the beads slightly and apply a dab of Zap-A-Gap to the spot on the wire where the bead will go. Move the bead back over the Zap-A-Gap and hold in place. Repeat for each tile.

step 10

MARK PLACING FOR HOUR SPOKES

Make a three-layer stack out of black clay rolled through the pasta machine at the thickest setting. Use the clay roller to mesh the layers together. Place the clock working onto the center of this circle, trace around it and cut out a circle for the clock hands. Bake and flatten the clay piece while cooling. Divide the clay circle into 12 equal spaces and make a mark at the edge of each space on the clay piece. You may use a purchased clock face as a template to make the spacing easy.

step 11

ATTACH TILE SPOKES TO CLOCK FACE

Carefully drill holes in the baked small circle with a pin vise. Lay out all of the tiles in the order you'd like to have them on the clock. Use Zap-A-Gap to attach the spoked tiles to the 3½" (9cm) black circle.

step 12

ATTACH SPOKED ASSEMBLAGE TO CLOCK FACE

Score the back of the clay face with a craft knife. Use Zap-A-Gap to attach the spoked assemblage to the baked clock face, taking care to align the slots where the clock mechanism will fit. Hold it in place for a few seconds to allow the glue to set.

step 13

PREPARE GOLD CLAY CIRCLE FOR CLOCK FRONT

Run a piece of gold clay through the pasta machine at the thickest setting. Use a compass to score a 3¾" (10cm) circle onto the gold clay. Cut out the circle with a craft knife and punch a hole in the center with a circle clay cutter that's big enough to accommodate the nut on the front of the clock mechanism. Stamp the circle, and then apply mica and embossing powders to it.

step 14

INSERT CLOCK WORKING AND ADHERE GOLD CIRCLE

Insert the clock working into the cut-out center of the clock. Apply dots of Zap-A-Gap around the small black piece and adhere the gold circle.

step 15

FINISH CLOCK

Attach the clock hands.

Raku Wrist Ring **I couldn't help it! I had to make these tiles into a bracelet! Note the difference between the tiles in the step-outs and the tiles on this bracelet. After I applied all the mica powder and heated the embossing powders, I used a foiling adhesive to apply colored foil to the surface. Just another little touch that you can do to make your friends wonder how you did that!**

materials

pale green polymer clay

copper polymer clay

Liquid Polyclay

glass pie dish

small word rubber stamp
(HERO ARTS)

square and swirl rubber stamps

black inkpad **(STAZON)**

green and gold mica powder

copper acrylic paint

Repel Gel

paintbrushes

craft knife

medium and small circle cutters

tissue blade

clay shaper

featured
technique

**simply
impressive**

Coffee Table
Wisdom

The small word stamp used under the copper layer of clay in this project says, "let what you love be what you do." Amen to that one! What secret message of wisdom would you like to telegraph? There are lots of clay cutters in different shapes, so instead of circles you could display your wisdom under windows of another style. This plate is for decorative purposes only and is not meant for food consumption or food display.

step1

BRUSH REPEL GEL OVER GLASS PIE PLATE

Brush Repel Gel over the entire inside of the glass pie plate with a paintbrush.

step2

PRESS GREEN CLAY INTO PIE PLATE

Condition and roll out a rectangular slab of pale green clay to a medium thickness on the pasta machine. Place the clay rectangle down the middle of the pie plate and press it into shape.

step3

STAMP GREEN CLAY

Trim the sides and edges of the rectangle with a tissue blade to a size that fits the pie plate. Carefully remove the clay and use black ink to stamp the phrase stamp all over the clay slab. Replace the green piece into the pie plate.

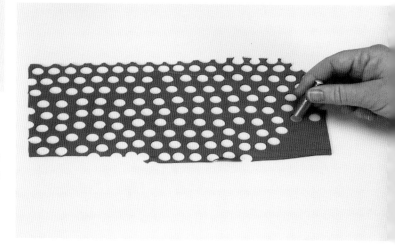

step4

PUNCH HOLES IN COPPER CLAY

Roll out a slab of copper clay to a medium thickness on the pasta machine. Use the medium-small circle cutter to punch holes all over the slab.

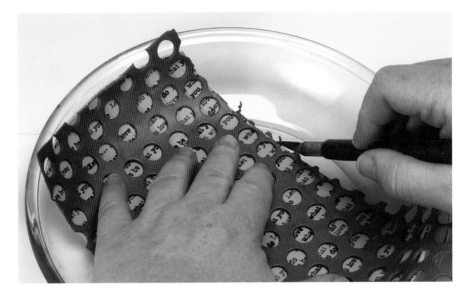

step 5

LAYER COPPER CLAY OVER GREEN CLAY

Cover the green clay with the perforated sheet of copper clay and trim the edges to match the edges of the green piece of clay.

step 6

PLACE ALL CLAY PIECES AND STAMP

Roll two sheets of green clay on a medium-thick setting on the pasta machine. Place one sheet on either side of the center sheet of green clay overlaid with the copper sheet. Trim the sheets to fit. Stamp all over the sheets with the uninked squares stamp.

step 7

COVER SEAMS AND TEXTURIZE

Roll out two thin coils of copper clay and press each one over the seams. Use the small rubber stamp to texturize the strips.

step 8

APPLY MICA POWDERS TO CLAY

Use your fingers or a brush to apply gold and green mica powders over the clay.

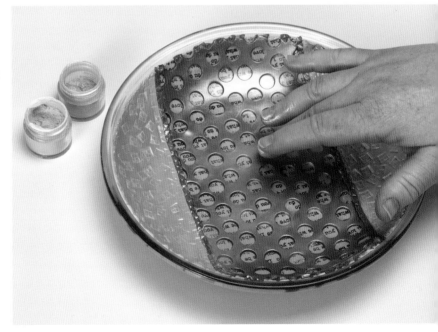

step 9

PAINT CLAY

Dilute copper acrylic paint with water and brush it over the pale green pieces of clay. Let it dry completely. Bake the plate at 275°F (135°C) for 15 minutes. While the piece is still warm, carefully remove the clay from the pie plate. Let the clay cool completely.

step 10

DECORATE BACK SIDE OF DISH

Roll a thin slab of clay at the thinnest setting on the pasta machine. Use the small circle cutter to punch holes into the slab. Brush the bottom of the dish with Liquid Polyclay. Use the positive and negative circle cut-outs to cover the bottom of the dish in a random manner. Stamp some of the positive circle cut-outs with a small swirl stamp. Rebake the dish at 250°F (121°C) for 15 minutes.

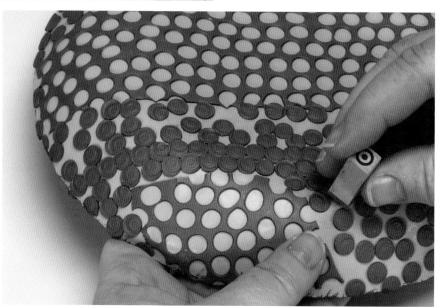

step 11

DECORATE EDGES OF PLATE

Paint the edges of the clay dish with copper paint and let it dry.

Resources

Most of the supplies used to make the projects in this book can be found in your local craft, hobby, bead or discount department stores. If you have trouble locating a specific product, contact one of the supply sources listed below to find a local or Internet vendor, or to request a catalog.

General Crafting Supplies

Here is a list of all the manufacturers who make the supplies used in this book. You'll find resources for everything from clay and inks to wire and beads.

BEACON ADHESIVES, INC.
125 MacQuesten Parkway South,
Mt. Vernon, NY 10550
(914) 699-3405
www.beacon1.com
my favorite glues

CLEARSNAP, INC.
P.O. Box 98,
Anacortes, WA 98221
(888) 448-4862
www.clearsnap.com
inks, stamps and lots of other
fun stuff

THE LEATHER FACTORY
703 Texas St.,
Houston, TX 77002
(281) 208-9293
leather and cool tools and findings

LISA PAVELKA'S HEART IN HAND STUDIO
9825 Tarzana Ln.,
Las Vegas, NV 89117
(702) 765-5471
www.heartinhandstudio.com
Poly Bonder glue and other polymer
clay accessories

PLAID ENTERPRISES, INC.
3225 Westech,
Norcross, GA 30092
(800) 842-4197
www.plaidonline.com
acrylic paints, All Night Media stamps,
general craft supplies

POLYFORM PRODUCTS CO.
1901 Estes Ave.,
Elk Grove Village, IL 60007
(847) 427-0020
www.sculpey.com
polymer clay

PRAIRIE CRAFT COMPANY
P.O. Box 209,
Florissant, CO 80816-0209
(719) 748-5110
www.prairiecraft.com
Kato Clay and polymer clay products

RANGER INDUSTRIES, INC.
15 Park Rd.,
Tinton Falls, NJ 07724
(732) 389-3535
www.rangerink.com
inkpads, embossing powders

STAEDTLER, INC.
21900 Plummer St.,
Chatsworth, CA 91311
(800) 776-5544
www.staedtler-usa.com
crayons, markers, pencils, cutting mats

SUZE WEINBERG DESIGN STUDIO, INC.
1301 W. Park Ave.,
Ocean, NJ 07712
(732) 493-1390
www.schmoozewithsuze.com
ultra-thick embossing powder

THINK INK
332 NE 162nd St.,
Shoreline, WA 98155
(800) 778-1935
www.thinkink.net
embossing powders

TSUKINEKO, INC.
17640 NE Sixty-fifth St.,
Redmond, WA 98052
(425) 883-7733
www.tsukineko.com
pens and inks

VISUAL IMAGE PRINTERY (VIP)
1215 N. Grove St.,
Anaheim, CA 92806
foils, spray webbing

WOODWORKS, LTD.
4521 Anderson Blvd.,
Fort Worth, TX 76117
(800) 722-0311
www.craftparts.com
wooden beads

Stamp Companies

Below I've listed all of the manufacturers who produce the stamps I used in this book. But these companies are just a sampling of what's available. If you want to find literally millions more stamps, simply type "rubber stamps" into an Internet search engine and you'll enter an alternate universe of stamps.

HERO ARTS
1343 Powell St.,
Emeryville, CA 94608
(800) 822-4376
www.heroarts.co

IMPRESS ME
17116 Escalon Dr.,
Encino, CA 91436-4030
(818) 788-6730
www.impressmenow.com

JUDI·KINS
17803 South Harvard Blvd.,
Gardena, CA 90248
(310) 515-1115
www.judikins.com

MAGENTA
2275 Bombardier,
Sainte-Julia, Quebec J3E 2J9, Canada
(450) 922-5253
www.magentastyle.com

POSH IMPRESSIONS
22600-A Lambert St., Suite 706,
Lake Forest, CA 92630
(800) 421-7674
www.poshimpressions.com

POST MODERN DESIGN
P.O. Box 720416,
Norman, OK 73070
(405) 321-3716

STAMP OASIS
5000 W. Oakey Blvd., Suite 17,
Las Vegas, NV 89146
(702) 880-8886
www.stampoasis.com

STAMPOTIQUE ORIGINALS
9822 N. 7th St.
Phoenix, AZ 85020
www.stampotique.com

Magazines

There are lots of fabulous magazines out there that are great to look at for getting new ideas and for being inspired by the creativity of others. Here are a few of my favorites.

RUBBERSTAMPMADNESS
P.O. Box 610,
Corvallis, OR 97339-0610
(877) 782-6762
www.rsmadness.com

STAMPINGTON & COMPANY
22992 Mill Creek, Ste. B,
Laguna Hills, CA 92653
(877) 782-6737
Publisher of *Belle Armoire*, *Somerset Studio*, *The Stamper's Sampler*, *Stampington Inspirations* and more!
www.stampington.com

EXPRESSION
Publisher's Development Corp.
12345 World Trade Dr.,
San Diego, CA 92128
www.expressionartmagazine.com

THE RUBBER STAMPER
published by Hobby Publications, Inc.
P.O. Box 102,
Morganville, NJ 07751
(800) 260-9028
www.rubberstamper.com

THE STUDIO ZINE
**This magazine is no longer published, but you can look at some of it online (plus other great stuff) at Teesha and Tracy Moore's website: www.teeshamoore.com

VAMP STAMP NEWS
P.O. Box 386,
Hanover, MD 21076-0386
www.vampstampnews.com

And check out my new DVD too!
Fabricadabra: Material Magic with Sandra McCall
PageSage
580 Crespi Dr., Ste. #A6-216,
Pacifica, CA 94044
www.pagesage.com

Index

Check out these other
North Light titles
for more great crafting ideas!

Bead on a Wire

by Sharilyn Miller

In this book, magazine editor and popular author Sharilyn Miller shows crafters of all levels how to get in on the popularity of jewelry and beading. Inside *Bead on a Wire*, you'll find an in-depth section on design and construction techniques that make it a snap to get started. You'll love to make the 20 step-by-step bead and wire jewelry projects, including gorgeous earrings, necklaces, brooches and bracelets. You'll be amazed at how easy it is to start making fashionable jewelry that's guaranteed to inspire compliments.

ISBN-13: 978-1-58180-650-2
ISBN-10: 1-58180-650-7
paperback, 128 pages, 33239

30 Minute Rubber Stamp Workshop

by Sandra McCall

Create a wonderful, personal gift in the time it takes to drive to the store! In *30 Minute Rubber Stamp Workshop*, Sandra McCall shows you how to handcraft gorgeous rubber-stamped pieces without taking all day to do it. The time-saving tips and pre-chosen color combinations in the book will help you cut down on prep time and make projects fly out of your fingers. This must-have book features 30 quick and easy projects, including 11 wearable gifts such as pins, necklaces and bracelets. Just follow the full-color illustrations and clear, step-by-step instructions, and you'll be making wonderful creations in no time.

ISBN-13: 978-1-58180-271-9
ISBN-10: 1-58180-271-4
paperback, 128 pages, 32142

Polymer Clay for the Fun of It

by Kim Cavender

As every polymer person knows, working with polymer clay is all about having fun and making great stuff. With its over 20 bright and colorful projects and variations, *Polymer Clay for the Fun of It!* shows readers how to have a good time with polymer clay. The book gives readers a comprehensive and lighthearted polymer clay "primer" along with a detailed techniques section to make getting started fun and easy. As a bonus feature, readers get "Just for the fun of it" tips to keep them inspired. Each project begins with an often tongue-in-cheek quote that matches the easygoing tone of the book. With *Polymer Clay for the Fun of It!* you can throw all of the rules out the window and just, well, have fun!

ISBN-13: 978-1-58180-684-7
ISBN-10: 1-58180-684-1
paperback, 128 pages, 33320

Art Stamping Workshop

by Gloria Page

Create a signature look with stamped images you carve yourself! *Art Stamping Workshop* introduces you to the world of carving and printing soft blocks to create great gifts, home décor items and personal apparel—all with a look uniquely yours. Detailed instructions on carving tools and techniques get you started. Then you'll learn to create 20 projects on paper, fabric and alternative surfaces, such as wood and polymer clay. Templates for recreating all stamp designs featured in the projects are included. Carving your own stamps gives you the freedom to use any image at any size and sets your work apart from the crowd. Discover the fulfillment that comes from printing your own images and start carving your stamps today!

ISBN-13: 978-1-58180-696-0
ISBN-10: 1-58180-696-5
paperback, 128 pages, 33355

THESE AND OTHER FINE NORTH LIGHT TITLES ARE AVAILABLE FROM YOUR LOCAL ART AND CRAFT RETAILER, BOOKSTORE OR ONLINE SUPPLIER.